1/98

Our Movie Heritage

Our Movie Heritage

Tom Mc Greevey
Joanne L. Yeck

Rutgers University Press
New Brunswick, New Jersey, and London

Library of Congress Cataloging-in-Publication Data

Mc Greevey, Tom.
     Our movie heritage / Tom Mc Greevey and Joanne L. Yeck.
       p. cm.
     Includes bibliographical references and index.
     ISBN 0-8135-2431-8 (alk. paper)
     1. Motion picture film—Preservation—United States.   I. Yeck, Joanne Louise.   II. Title.
TR886.3.M37   1997
778.5'8'0973—dc21   97-3737
                                                              CIP

British Cataloging-in-Publication data for this book is available from the British Library

"Academy Award(s)®" and "Oscar®" are registered trademarks and service marks of the Academy of Motion Picture Arts and Sciences ("A.M.P.A.S."). The copyrighted Award of Merit ("Oscar") statuette is identified as "copr. A.M.P.A.S. 1941." The depiction of the "Oscar" statuette is also a registered trademark and service mark of A.M.P.A.S. In addition, the "Oscar" statuette and depictions thereof are trade names of A.M.P.A.S.

Designed and typeset by Ellen C. Dawson

Manufactured in the United States of America

To Willa and John, who knew the magic of Ingrid Bergman's smile,
and to Zan, who has yet to discover it

Contents

Foreword
Leonard Maltin

Millions of Americans took their children to see the *Star Wars* trilogy when it returned to theaters in 1997. They wanted to relive a special experience in their moviegoing lives—and share it with their kids.

But when George Lucas examined the negatives of his megahit movies—no more than twenty years old—he was dismayed to discover how badly they had deteriorated. It required a great deal of technological know-how, TLC, and money to make new prints that looked right to the demanding filmmaker.

This, more than any recent example I could cite, underscores the crisis nature of film preservation. If *Star Wars* is in jeopardy, what is the status of early Edison shorts, or Chaplin comedies made sixty to seventy years earlier?

Just because a film exists on videotape, simply because it's shown on cable television, doesn't mean it's been saved. This is the toughest concept to get across to the average person. Films were meant to be shown in theaters—from *Singin' in the Rain* to *The Empire Strikes Back*—and if the negatives and prints don't exist in superior condition, that simply isn't possible.

Everybody, or so it seems, likes to go to the movies. Cinema is the most democratic art form of our time, crossing over every conceivable ethnic, social, and geographic boundary line. Yet the enormous popularity of movies has also proven to be something of a curse—because—because people take them for granted. After all, they're just movies.

Even after several supposedly enlightened decades of film scholarship and growing public awareness of cinema as art, movies still have to fight to be taken seriously alongside painting, music, and literature.

What is more—and what is worse—they turn out to be as fragile as any canvas or manuscript. Indeed, the parchment on which the Declaration of Independence was written, and the fabric on which Winslow Homer painted some of his most famous images, have already lasted longer than any motion picture ever made. Those American artifacts, well kept and watched over, will survive into the twenty-first century. Thousands of American films, made during the equivalent of a lifetime, have already vanished.

Millions of feet of unprotected newsreel film, an invaluable record of our life and times, sit waiting for funding so they can be copied and saved for future generations. If an old newspaper was starting to crumble, a librarian would immediately copy it onto microfilm. At the very least, he or she could photocopy it and save a representation of the original.

Films require much more care, and much more money, to protect. Everyone I know agrees that "it should be done," but no one is quite sure how to raise the necessary funds before time runs out. Once a negative has deteriorated, it cannot be brought back to life.

Before there can be funds, there has to be concern, and concern will not come without education. That is why I am so glad that Joanne Yeck and Tom Mc Greevey have undertaken this project, to celebrate our American film heritage, and underscore its fragile nature.

Movies speak to us on such a personal level, they become a part of our lives. We relate them to special moments, like a first date. We want to pass them on to our children.

Preserving American films—from turn-of-the-century newsreels to *The Godfather*—should be everyone's concern. It is not a matter of corporate investment, but cultural continuity.

I celebrate this book, as it in turn celebrates our American film heritage. I hope it succeeds in raising some consciousness—and perhaps, raising some funds—to keep these movies alive.

Acknowledgments

This book is the end result of a love affair with the movies. It began in the darkness of a variety of movie theaters, starting in 1947 in the run-down, "continuous showing," former legitimate theaters on Forty-second Street in New York and in 1967 when *Gone With the Wind* played in a suburban theater in Dayton, Ohio.

It is a love that continues to this day.

So, first we wish to thank the moviemakers—the men and women who created the moving images that captured our hearts. Without them there wouldn't be a first hundred years of motion pictures, and there wouldn't be *Our Movie Heritage*.

The second group to whom we owe thanks are our families, teachers, neighbors, friends, classmates and co-workers who shared and fostered our enthusiasm for the movies. No book writes itself, and to everybody who helped with this one we say: "We couldn't have done it without you."

We're grateful to several individuals at the Library of Congress who gave us support and guidance—David Francis for his encouragement and enthusiasm; Steve Leggett, who never tired of answering one more question; Dina Fleming; and Ken Weissman, who contributed both his time and expertise again and again.

Other specialists in the field who gave their valuable time for this book were Leith Adams, Mary Lea Bandy, Susan Dalton, Michael Friend, Robert Gitt, Chris Horak, Jim Katz, Scott MacQueen, Gil O'Gara, Tony Slide, Paul Spehr, Paolo Cherchi Usai, and especially Robert Harris, who embraced our project and opened doors for us.

For helping us through the labyrinth of still permissions, our thanks to: Margaret Adamic, Grover Crisp, Douglas Fairbanks, Jr., Rebecca Herrera, Paul Jarrico, Peter Langs, Kathy Lendech, Larry McCallister, Margarita Medina, Debra Mostow, Ken Ross, Jennifer Sebree, Judith Singer, Frederick Wiseman, and Pattie Withers.

Our thanks to everyone who generously donated photographs: The American Film Institute, American Movie Classics, Cinesite, Bill Everson, David Francis, George

Eastman House, Robert Harris, Fay Kanin, Los Angeles County Museum of Art, Roger Mayer, Museum of Modern Art, National Center for Film and Video Preservation, Paul Spehr, Bruce Thomson, Underground Vault & Storage, Inc., Ken Weissman, and Robert Wise.

Thanks to Deane Johnson for his sympathetic ear and permission to use the still from *A Streetcar Named Desire;* to Peter Benchley and The Robert Benchley Estate; to The Bette Davis Estate; to The Harold Lloyd Estate and First Interstate Bank; and to Matty Kemp for the Mary Pickford Company.

We're grateful for lots of help with important photo research: Eddie Brandt's Saturday Matinee; Tom Barnett (Cinema Collectors); Nancy Blaine and Nikki Martinez (The American Film Institute); Ann and Paddy Calistro; Ernie and Roberta Bohem (Photoreporters); Cornelia Emerson (The UCLA Film and Television Archive); Jeff Gainey (Iconographics); Joe Garza; Terry Geesken, Graham Leggat, and Mary-Anne Smith (Museum of Modern Art); Lauren Gibson; Janet Lorenz (NFIS/Academy of Motion Picture Arts and Sciences); Janice Madhu and Rebecca Wehle (George Eastman House); Linda Montoya (LM Images); Jayne Wallace; and especially, The Ohio Book Store Collection.

We also want to thank the staffs at the Margaret Herrick Library (Academy of Motion Picture Arts and Sciences); the Santa Fe Public Library; and The E. E. Fogelson Library Center at the College of Santa Fe, as well as Greer Garson and E. E. "Buddy" Fogelson, whose generous bequests have fostered film studies in Santa Fe.

Love to our friends and family, Janice Ballard, Sam Berne, Alton Christensen, James Gauer, Katy Mc Greevey, Anna Merlan, Nancy Nelson, Bob Schrei, and Aura Walker, whose support kept us healthy and happy during the book's long gestation period.

The careful reading of the manuscript by Eric Aijala, John Belton, David Francis, Bob Gitt, Robert Harris, Steve Leggett, Pete Lindeman, Janet Lorenz, Susan Reyburn, Ken Weissman and John Yeck resulted in a better book. And especially, thanks to Rudy Behlmer, whose fine-toothed comb found many overlooked flaws.

A number of authors and journalists have been dedicated to keeping the cause of film preservation in front of the public. Their conscientious reporting and scholarship were vital to this book. Particular thanks to Annette Melville and Scott Simmon who summarized the Library of Congress's *Film Preservation 1993*, Kevin Brownlow, Cornelia Emerson, Bill Everson, Bob Fisher, Ron Haver, Joseph McBride, Dennis Wharton, and, especially, Anthony Slide, whose detailed and ground-breaking study of film preservation in *Nitrate Won't Wait* gave this project an invaluable springboard.

Many thanks to Buckley Jeppson and The Preservation Press who first believed in the project. And our deepest gratitude to all the wonderful people at Rutgers University Press and especially to our editor Leslie Mitchner, who loves the movies as much as we do.

And, thanks to Leonard Maltin who found time in his busy schedule to express his care and concern for our movie heritage in the foreword to this book.

Lastly, our gratitude goes to Olivia de Havilland, without whose kindness, support, and encouragement, the movies might have been a passing fancy.

Our Movie Heritage

There's nothing like it.

You're sitting in a theater filled with excited people. The lights dim. The "click, click, click" of the projector begins. An image bursts onto a screen.

Charlie Chaplin eating his shoe . . . Greta Garbo by candlelight . . . Errol Flynn's dazzling smile . . . Ginger Rogers's twirling skirt . . . Rita Hayworth's flaming red hair . . . Stanley Kubrick's vision of the year 2001.

Indelible images like these emotionally captivating moments are priceless historical records that right now are steadily slipping away.

The movies capture an extraordinary personal and collective history of the American people. They also reveal the history of an art form that created an industry. The films themselves are significant and unique cultural documents of the twentieth century, containing irreplaceable sights *and* sounds of our past.

These movies are disappearing because motion picture film is by nature self-destructive. Whether it's a piece of cellulose nitrate exposed in 1910 or a strip of Eastman Color acetate stock produced in the 1970s—*all* film self-destructs. And, whether it steadily crumbles to dust or consumes itself in a fiery blaze, it self-destructs at a *very* rapid rate.

Today, the movies of the past are an endangered species. These fragile records of the twentieth century require expert and prompt attention. If we are to preserve our movie heritage for future generations, it must be done now.

"Every film is a time capsule which tells us how we saw ourselves, and how others saw us, at a point in our past. The disappearance of a film or archival videotape is therefore not only a loss of an artistic object, it is also a partial obliteration of our nation's history.

"It is unthinkable that our children will grow up into a world so bland that their visions will no longer be tantalized by the colors of Renoir or Chagall. It should be equally unthinkable that our children could inhabit a world no longer enlarged and defined by the artistry of Chaplin, the vision of Orson Welles, the magic of Méliès.

"But, if Mozart and Keats have their protectors, Chaplin and Welles may well fade into something less than memory. Our task is to keep this from happening."
—Frank Hodsoll,
former chairman, National
Endowment for the Arts

Our Vanishing Cinematic Past

This is the first century to have been preserved on film . . . maybe.
—Dustin Hoffman

In the beginning, film was made of *cellulose nitrate*—"nitrate" for short. Its use dominated moviemaking until the 1950s. Nitrate film gave photography a full range of vivid, shimmering blacks and whites and grays. It produced the dramatic light and shadow in some of America's most important movies, from *The Birth of a Nation* (1915) to *Citizen Kane* (1941).

With the advent of the three-strip Technicolor process in the late 1930s, nitrate served the full-color spectrum just as well, capturing the rich, red earth of Georgia in *Gone With the Wind* (1939) and the painterly scenes of *Meet Me in St. Louis* (1944).

In addition to its superb photographic abilities, however, nitrate has other, far less desirable properties. The chemical nature of nitrate film is unstable, **"Nitrate Won't Wait"** its elements constantly acting on each other to alter the composition of the whole. A reel of nitrate film in a can is a literal time bomb waiting to explode or more often, and much less dramatically, quietly to turn to dust.

Stored in a can, in the dark of a vault, cellulose nitrate undergoes a metamorphosis. It steadily decomposes through several stages until the image and the sound track vanish, and what is left turns to powder.

During this process, nitrate-based motion picture film becomes extremely volatile, turning into the equivalent of nitroglycerine in a film can. It is combustible and highly explosive; its "cousin"—*fully* nitrated cellulose—is actually used for explosives.

It is also highly flammable. One element of nitrate's chemical makeup is oxygen. As nitrate film burns, the oxygen is released, fanning the flames, thus making a nitrate fire nearly impossible to extinguish.

For theater owners and audiences, the projection of nitrate prints always carried with it the threat of fire and explosion. Between the advent of the movies at the end of

A major star of the 1920s, Colleen Moore made more than fifty feature films and outlived most of them; the majority have crumbled and disappeared.
Photo: The Museum of Modern Art/Film Stills Archive.

the nineteenth century and the middle of the twentieth century, nitrate film fires and explosions had resulted in hundreds of disasters.

A June 27, 1914, story from *The Moving Picture World* reveals the tremendous, explosive power of a vault full of film in cans.

> The explosion came about 10 o'clock in the morning without the slightest warning. No one was in the vault at the time and that it was tightly closed up is given as the reason for the force of the let-go which was sufficient to blow out an entire wall of brick and concrete eighteen inches thick.
> Brick and mortar were blown in every direction and a string of two-story houses on the same street were badly damaged, some of them being practically destroyed.

Rolls of burning film were showered everywhere and many of the adjoining buildings were set on fire. It was fire that injured the Italian boy who is not expected to recover; he was playing in the street near the vault at the time of the explosion and his clothes were ignited by a roll of film.

A large chunk of film history went up in flames in Little Ferry, New Jersey, on July 9, 1937, when a massive nitrate fire and explosion destroyed most of the silent films produced by Fox Film Corporation. Anthony Slide in *Nitrate Won't Wait* described the inferno:

Flames from the blast shot over 100 feet in the air and the same distance horizontally over the ground. A thirteen-year-old boy living with his family in a house immediately in front of the film storage vaults was killed while shielding his mother from the blast, which destroyed 42 individual vaults, in which the majority of silent films produced by Fox were stored. Following the fire, 57 truckloads of burned nitrate film were salvaged for their silver content, with each can of film ashes said to be worth approximately five cents.

Nitrate film can spontaneously combust at the relatively low temperature of 105° F and burn at the phenomenal rate of twenty tons in three minutes. This destruction was caused by a nitrate fire in the 1920s.
Photo: The Academy of Motion Picture Arts and Sciences.

In addition to nitrate's explosive quality, it deteriorates rapidly in hot and humid temperatures. In these conditions, it can quickly become useless, even before decomposition makes it dangerous.

In 1915 the motion picture magazine *Motography* carried an editorial entitled "Can Films Be Preserved for Posterity?" It described a British experiment in which film was stored—unused and untouched—in an airtight vault. After only five years, the stock inside was covered with a fungus. Apparently, this discovery was not widely noted or was ignored by filmmakers and those responsible for storing film.

In the early days, most of the motion picture industry saw little value in saving old film that was dangerous and expensive to store. "Posterity" was not a concern, since during the nitrate-era there were no ancillary markets such as television or videocassette. Once a film had had its run in the theaters, most producers considered its exhibition life over and its value nil.

Motion picture studios and independent producers also regularly destroyed prints to prevent them from being copied. In the days of silent films, illegal duplication—or "piracy"—was a perpetual problem. Because the images did not depend on sound, stolen movies could be recut, retitled, and reissued. The actual owner had little or no recourse against the film pirate.

Additionally, films were sometimes destroyed to retrieve the silver used to make the nitrate stock. Fledgling pioneer producers operating on shoestring budgets would sell used film for the silver content to help finance their next picture.

With all of these factors working against posterity, less than half of the twenty-one thousand feature-length American films made before 1950 still exist today.

Many were saved in a variety of ways and for a variety of reasons, although even those films that survived were largely ignored and often forgotten. Left in their cans—

A reel of nitrate film in a can is a literal time bomb waiting to explode. More often, and much less dramatically, the last stage of decomposition is a fine, brownish dust. *Photo: The Academy of Motion Picture Arts and Sciences.*

As nitrate film deterioration advances, the film becomes soft and sticky. Blisters form and the film starts to ooze a brown gummy liquid. Gas bubbles give off a noticeable odor. As bad as it looks, part of this reel can still be saved.
Photo: The Museum of Modern Art/Film Stills Archive.

unchecked and uncared for—many burned or steadily turned to dust as the years passed.

Decomposition is progressive. If noticed early enough, a film can be restored and transferred to safer acetate or polyester-based stocks. Otherwise, the film tends first to become brittle and shrink. The images fade and discolor. Next, the film becomes soft and sticky. Blisters form, and the film starts to ooze a brown gummy liquid that preservationists call "honey." This congeals into a solid mass and finally disintegrates into a pile of red dust.

Once decomposition begins, nitrate film is capable of spontaneous combustion at the relatively low temperature of 105°F. It can burn at the phenomenal rate of twenty tons in three minutes.

In 1983 Audrey Kupferberg, then archivist for the American Film Institute, described the shock of finding totally decomposed footage. "*Angel of Contention* was such a film. When we got it there weren't more than two frames that had an image left. You have to junk the film outright. There is powder, gel, but no film."

No one knows exactly how many nitrate titles have already disappeared, never to be viewed again, but the survival rate of those produced before the mid-1920s is extremely low. Recent statistics estimate that 10 percent of the feature films made between 1910 and 1920 survive, and an only slightly higher 20 percent from the 1920s still exist.

With the advent of sound in 1927 and under the management of the major studios, movies received better care. New research shows that close to 90 percent of the feature films from the 1930s have survived in some form.

For many significant silent films, however, there are no known existing negatives or prints. Movies that starred some of the most popular actors and actresses of their day, such as Greta Garbo in *The Divine Woman* (1928), may never be seen again. *Angel of Contention* (1919) starring Lillian Gish, Theda Bara's *Cleopatra* (1917), Rudolph Valentino's *The Young Rajah* (1922), and Gloria Swanson's *Madame Sans-Gêne* (1925) are all presumed lost.

Silent "vamp" Theda Bara's *Cleopatra* (1917) is one of the important lost American films.

Although these films may be gone, some even earlier ones are still available and preservable. These include many of America's first films that survived the ravages of time through a quirk in the copyright law.

These films were discovered in the early 1940s by a young man named Howard Walls who was working at the Library of Congress. Walls found a vault in the main building that had not been opened for twenty-five years; the lock had to be sawed off in order to open the massive iron door. Behind the door was a treasure trove of early silent films dating from the inception of motion pictures in 1893. Walls had uncovered the Library's "forgotten" collection of *paper prints*—more than three thousand films produced prior to 1918.

There had been no provision for copyrighting motion pictures on film before 1912. Since protection could only be obtained for still photographs, motion picture producers printed every frame of their negatives onto paper and deposited these "paper prints" with the Library. Paper prints were still being submitted as late as 1917, and the result was the enormous collection discovered by Walls. In this long-ignored vault were the frame-by-frame paper versions of the works of great motion picture pioneers such as Thomas Edison and the filmmakers at Biograph and Keystone, home of "The Keystone Kops."

The Young Rajah (1922), starring Rudolph Valentino, and *Madame Sans-Gêne* (1925), starring Gloria Swanson, are only two of America's "lost" films.
Photos: Courtesy, Paramount Pictures.

There is no existing print of Greta Garbo's film *The Divine Woman* (1928). The majority of her films, however, are well preserved at George Eastman House.

To transfer these prints onto film stock so they could be viewed, Walls enlisted the help of Carl Gregory, a motion picture engineer at the National Archives. Gregory took an optical printer—a device that both projects and photographs at the same time—and modified it to copy the paper prints. The work had to be halted during World War II before much progress had been made.

In the early 1950s Kemp Niver, an inventive former Los Angeles policeman, developed what he called "The Renovare Process"—a technique for transferring the paper images, frame by frame, on to 16mm film through the use of an overhead camera. His device and his dogged determination to copy the paper prints won Niver an honorary Academy Award in 1955.

Although successfully copied to film, the quality was less than ideal. So in 1983

Many pre-1917 movies that might have been lost to decomposing nitrate are preserved at the Library of Congress thanks to frame-by-frame paper versions of the originals.
Photo by Ken Weissman.

the UCLA Film and Television Archive, working with the Library of Congress, began the retransfer of the paper prints to 35mm and that project is now being carried forward at the Library's conservation center in Dayton, Ohio.

The transfer of the paper prints back to celluloid was a boon of considerable proportion to historians interested in the infancy of the American cinema. The period from 1913 to 1924 has not fared as well, however, and from those ten years only a very small fraction of the films produced have survived.

Film historian William K. Everson explains in his book *American Silent Film:*

> Most of the *obviously* important films of 1921 (to take a date at random) are still with us: Fairbanks's *The Three Musketeers,* Germany's *The Cabinet of Dr. Caligari,* and France's *J'Accuse* . . . Chaplin's *The Kid.* . . . Yet a thorough perusal of one

of the trade papers of 1921 shows that no less than 525 films were released that year.

. . . Out of those 525 films, only about 50 are known to exist today—the more important ones generally available throughout the world's archives, but many of the others represented only by a single print in a studio vault or in the hands of a private collector.

. . . The story is repeated every year [for the decade of the 1920s], although from 1925 on the proportion of salvaged and preserved films is, happily, somewhat higher.

Not all nitrate footage was created equal. For example, during World War II, standards of film processing suffered because of material shortages. Similarly, the color tinting of silent films sometimes compromised their stability. And a surprising element added to the rapid deterioration of silent films—the intertitle.

Sometimes referred to as title cards, intertitles are the printed cards inserted into silent films to tell what is being said and to describe story transitions. Because they carried only words, these strips of film required less exact developing than the images in the dramatic scenes. As a result, they often received less attention from the laboratories. Inadequate processing of these negatives hastened their decay and that of the film around them.

Archives often removed titles to save on storage space. An unexpected benefit of this practice was that the films whose titles were removed have had a much higher rate of survival. In *American Silent Film,* William Everson tells the story:

In many ways, removing the titles was an extremely wise course. The films thus pruned have survived in far better condition than the majority of prints that were not so treated. In the bulk of rediscovered decaying prints or negatives, the rotting sections can be traced directly back to the titles, the worst of the decomposition occurring *within* the title footage.

The Vinegar Syndrome   A rash of nitrate-caused fires in the late 1940s finally prompted the motion picture industry to abandon the use of cellulose nitrate. Its replacement was *cellulose triacetate,* commonly called "acetate," or "safety" because it doesn't have nitrate's explosive qualities. Safety film had been available to filmmakers since before World War I and had always been the material used for 16mm and 8mm film. It was, however, relatively costly and had inferior photographic capabilities.

Its most important qualities were that it was neither highly flammable nor combustible. In the early 1950s, the industry switched to acetate-based negatives and prints, ending the threat of fire and explosion for theater owners, projectionists, and moviegoers.

Since acetate was believed to be much more stable than nitrate, this seemed a giant step forward for the cause of film preservation as well. However, in recent years, when film archivists have opened stored cans containing acetate negatives or prints, they have been hit with the strong, rather familiar odor of sweaty gym shoes.

What they are smelling are the pungent fumes of acetic acid—olfactory evidence that "safety film," like its volatile predecessor nitrate, is subject to decomposition. And it is now known that as acetate-based film deteriorates, it cooks—literally stewing in its own juice. The higher the temperature and relative humidity, the faster the pot boils. This has been termed the "vinegar syndrome."

Technically speaking, according to Eastman Kodak, vinegar syndrome happens like this: "Cellulose triacetate results from a chemical reaction between cellulose and acetic acid. Acetate decomposition (or deacetylation) is the reverse reaction: the acetate ion reacts with moisture to form acetic acid. The acid produces the characteristic vinegar odor."

In 1993 during a hearing before a panel of the National Film Preservation Board, George Stevens, Jr., recalled the shock of finding that a thirty-two-year-old film directed by his father was already seriously compromised by the vinegar syndrome.

> When we were preserving films [in the 1960s at the AFI], we thought that res-
> cue work was about the silent films, the nitrate films, the films from the distant
> past. It never occurred to me that I would be getting a call in 1990 about a film
> made in 1958, *The Diary of Anne Frank.*
>
> Somebody from the Fox studio called and said that they had gone to the neg-
> ative—the only negative, the existing negative—of *The Diary of Anne Frank,* and
> found that two reels of the film had become "vinegarized."
>
> This film was made with such care, such beautiful photography and such
> beautiful lighting about a subject of such importance by an individual who
> believed that films well made would stand the test of time and be of interest
> to other generations.
>
> Fox was aware that I had a 35mm print of the film, and the sad conclusion
> of this was that the only way to re-create those two reels of *The Diary of Anne
> Frank* was to make a negative off the print. And, of course, that means that film
> will forever exist in a degraded state.

Vinegar syndrome has yet to be detected in films that have been duplicated under archival conditions and put into ideal storage immediately. However, separate studies concur that acetate may prove to have a shorter life than nitrate-based film. Today polyester-based film promises a significantly longer life than acetate. While George East-man House, the UCLA Film and Television Archive, and the National Archives, for example, have made some nitrate conversions onto polyester stocks, other archivists have hesitated to switch. This is in part because polyester requires some changes in preser-vation techniques, but mainly because of their experience with acetate safety film. Twenty or thirty years from now, archivists wonder, what will be discovered about the deteri-orating properties of polyester?

Pink Sand? The Problems of Eastman Color

Although all the evidence isn't in yet, it appears to be an inescapable conclusion that acetate is more short-lived than nitrate. Compounding this problem is the fact that Eastman Color negatives and prints fade and can lose their true color also much faster than nitrate decomposes.

During the 1940s, when most films were routinely shot in black and white, the lush hues of Technicolor were the industry's high-priced color standard. Technicolor required a bulky camera in which three black-and-white negatives were simultaneously exposed. Technicolor negatives involved no color dyes. In a process called "dye-transfer," the movies became colorful at the printing stage, much the same way full color is printed onto paper.

When Kodak introduced the less expensive and less complicated Eastman Color in the 1950s, it was widely welcomed, and its use gradually became the rule rather than the exception in Hollywood film production. The Eastman Kodak Company's "dye-coupler" color process, Eastman Color, had two distinct money-saving advantages over

Technicolor. It needed less light during photography, and it captured color on a single negative, making it easier to process.

However, because the stock contained the color, it was also subject to fading, and many of the earliest Eastman Color negatives and prints have already seriously deteriorated.

On October 26, 1979, the Los Angeles County Museum of Art showed *That Touch of Mink,* then a seventeen-year-old movie. Halfway through the film, as Cary Grant and Doris Day look out through French doors from a lavish, ocean-front hotel suite in Bermuda, Grant says, "Nowhere else in the world can you see beaches with pink sand."

The audience exploded with laughter.

The laughter in the museum theater was not because the sand wasn't pink, but because *everything* on the huge screen was pink: the sand, Grant's jacket, even Doris Day's hair! The film had been printed on unstable Eastman Color and had lost all but its pink-ish hues.

According to restoration expert Robert Harris, the camera negatives of nearly every Eastman Color film of the 1950s, as well as those made in the early 1960s, are already losing their true color. Musicals like *Oklahoma!* (1955), epics like *Spartacus* (1960), and realistic dramas like *Midnight Cowboy* (1969) are just as vulnerable as the nitrate films of the 1920s.

Like nitrate, Eastman Color films fade at varying rates. The quality of the original processing, when the original stock was manufactured, and the storage conditions all affect the speed of deterioration. Color fading is probably the most expensive preservation task faced today.

Fortunately, research at Eastman Kodak has already produced several improved lower-fading preprint and print color stocks. In 1981 Henry Kaska, the public information director at Kodak, responded to the flurry of questions about the color-fading crisis, saying, "We have the technology to prevent color film from fading but, thus far, Hollywood hasn't invested because they haven't seen the commercial value in it."

By the 1990s Hollywood had changed its mind, and contemporary films shot in color have a much brighter future. Currently, the best preventive medicine for filmmakers who film in Eastman Color is immediate cold/dry storage and the creation of black-and-white separation masters.

These "protection positives" separate the spectrum's three primary colors onto individual low-contrast positive prints. Like the Technicolor process, they do not contain the color and are not subject to fading. At one time only "significant" films such as *Star Wars* (1977), which would have a reissue life, were protected using this method. Today, separations are made routinely by some studios and sporadically by others.

A Herculean Task   Except for human negligence, physical wear-and-tear, and actual physical loss, the causes of deterioration in film are rooted in the very nature of the materials of which it is made: cellulosic plastics, nitrate and acetate, color dyes and silver.
                        —*James M. Reilly, director, Image Permanence Institute*

Today, few nitrate, acetate, or Eastman Color films decompose due to neglect. Many contemporary films immediately receive proper storage and protection. But for those films produced before the studios took a long-term interest in their product, lack of funds and trained personnel to restore and duplicate them still leads to tremendous annual losses.

In the early days, nitrate footage was often destroyed for its silver content and to protect producers from piracy. This photo, taken in 1922, shows an employee of the Douglas Fairbanks Studio chopping up "useless" film. *Photo: Courtesy, National Center for Film and Video Preservation.*

The exact cost of saving faded color and deteriorating nitrate and acetate isn't known. In January 1995 the cost of protecting needy film worldwide was estimated by the United Nations culture agency. UNESCO announced a staggering new statistic. "At least 10 percent of the 7.2 billion feet of film conserved in libraries throughout the world urgently needs restoration, at a cost of up to $1.7 billion."

About 100 million feet of that figure are American movies on nitrate waiting to be transferred and saved. Tens of thousands of feet of this film disappear annually. Although there is a great desire to preserve this decaying film, the number of unsalvageable titles grows every day.

Complicating this problem is the fact that most nitrate footage is not in the hands of its copyright owners. Rather it is in the hands of public archives that don't have the money to preserve it. Additionally, many of these titles are "orphans"—films without owners to pay for their preservation.

Film archives like the one at the University of California at Los Angeles periodically review and junk decomposing film in order to give other footage stored nearby or in the same can a better chance of survival. According to UCLA's preservation officer Robert

Gitt, there is even a special vault for the "hardship cases"—a sort of "death row" for disintegrating nitrate where the soon-to-be-dumped films spend their final days. Incarcerated there, awaiting their reprieve, languish significant titles like *Charley's Aunt* (1925), the comedy farce starring Charlie Chaplin's brother, Sydney Chaplin.

Time is of the essence. Film is as ephemeral as the light and shadow it creates on the screen. It isn't marble. It isn't even oil paint on canvas. If it is to last beyond its transitory lifetime, film must be preserved by duplicating it onto longer-lasting material. Much of the world's unique nitrate is on the edge of irreversible decomposition. Even with the preventative measures offered with cold/dry storage, film will not wait forever. *Now* is our best opportunity to save our movie heritage. Like an ancient piece of Native American pottery or the Declaration of Independence, American movies need protection from time and the elements. Funds, labor, talent, and dedication are required to save our cinematic past for the future. It will also take hundreds, perhaps thousands, of individuals who are convinced that movies are a unique cultural heritage worth saving and who are willing to help save it.

There is hope. There is a growing cooperation between public archives and studios to complete nitrate conversion, and increased communication among archivists, reducing duplication of efforts. Every remaining title may not be saved, but many will be. New technologies and better storage facilities will help archivists to better preserve and restore the films that are left.

There is also a wider awareness within the general public that movies are worth saving. For many films there is an eager and curious audience who find these celluloid treasures not only entertainment but also a gateway into America's past.

Director Francis Ford Coppola put it succinctly, "We love the films. And we love the young people. And we want them to have them." Saving film means that future generations will have an extraordinary and unique window on the twentieth century—the first century to be captured totally in moving images.

Saving the Movies:

America's Most Popular Art Form

For our century, film is at once an art form, a historical document, a cultural artifact, a market commodity, a political force, and an omnipresent object of popular culture.   *—Robert Rosen, director, UCLA Film and Television Archive*

Why bother to save movies?

Traditionally, as individuals and as a culture, we save things we value. We ought to save the best or most characteristic expressions of who we are as human beings and as a people. This is the rich value in the movies—a value that is clear to many, yet still unfolding and just being realized by others.

Most people think of movies as mere entertainment, but movies have had a multidimensional role in the twentieth century. In addition to providing entertainment, movies have recorded the variety of human culture and experience, our history and our fantasies. The story of the movies is much more than the story of a segment of the entertainment industry. The movies are irreplaceable artistic, cultural, and historic documents.

Never before in the world's history have we been able to see and hear how our forebears acted, thought, and spoke. According to Robert Rosen, director of the UCLA Film and Television Archive, some people are cynical about saving film: "They think most of it deserves to disappear." Rosen believes that there are several excellent reasons for saving film—film of all types:

> One is that film constitutes the preeminent popular art form of this century. It's also a document of our culture, recording not only what happened, but what we thought about what happened—not only the truths of the past seventy-five years, but also the mythologies, the misconceptions, the attitudes that were prevalent. In my own view, moving image media—film and TV—are this century's collective memory. To lose it is to lose part of ourselves.

The primary purpose of the Hollywood film was to entertain. Between the end of the nineteenth century, when simple short films were shown in nickelodeons, and the blossoming of television in the 1950s, millions of Americans grew up with the movies as a highly significant form of entertainment—and education.

From their earliest years motion pictures were a schoolroom for learning about the manners and mores of American life. During the silent era a significant percentage of moviegoers were immigrants. In darkened theaters these new Americans learned about life in their adopted land. In 1929 when dialogue became a permanent part of the movies, non–English-speaking Americans even learned their new language at the movies.

As early as 1909 theater critic Walter Eaton observed: "When you reflect that in New York City alone, on a Sunday 500,000 people go to the moving picture shows, a majority of them perhaps children . . . you cannot dismiss canned drama with a shrug of contempt. . . . Ten million people attended professional baseball games in America in 1908. Four million people attend moving picture theatres, it is said, every day." Even in 1909 movies were not just "canned drama," they were big business.

By the 1920s there were twenty thousand cinemas across the country. As many as ninety million tickets were sold every week. The film industry was one of the largest

Seen here in 1934, the Warner Bros.' Earle Theatre in Washington, D.C., offered movies and a stage show. Now renamed The Warner Theatre, the 1924 building, a designated District of Columbia landmark, has undergone a $10 million restoration, returning it to its former grandeur.
Photo: The Museum of Modern Art/Film Stills Archive.

businesses in the nation, with only basic necessities like food and clothing ahead of it.

Even the Great Depression of the 1930s could not cripple the motion picture industry. When sixteen million people were unemployed—about one-third of the available labor force—and many millions more were only partially employed, moviegoers still purchased seventy-five million tickets a week. Money was scarce, yet millions of Americans spent some of the little they had at the movies. They were buying the "magic"— the movies' ability to take audiences away from their everyday concerns. For many Depression-weary Americans, escaping into the fantasy world of the movies had truly become a basic necessity.

In 1930 the total U.S. population was 123 million. It is estimated that someone from the average household went to the movies three times a week. By 1941, when economic prosperity was returning, the U.S. population had grown to 132 million, and the annual movie attendance in the U.S. topped 2.8 billion. Going to the movies remained immensely popular throughout World War II and reached an all-time high in 1946.

During the 1930s and 1940s, "going to the movies" was a much fuller experience than it is in the 1990s. There were the trailers or "previews" of coming attractions and the feature film, as we have now. But there was also often some combination of the following: a second feature film, a newsreel, a short subject, a cartoon, and, in the big cities, live music and perhaps a stage show in place of the second feature.

For many people going to the movies was an *event* of more importance than the particular feature film that happened to be playing.

However, movies have always been more than entertainment and escape. The movies had a profound influence on those who saw them, shaping everything from fashion trends to moral values. For those like director Sydney Pollack, who grew up in the movie-going generation, their view of the world was often Hollywood's view. Pollack remembers:

> A lot of our own sense of morality. Our sense of romantic love. Our sense of virtue. What it is. How it's defined. Our sense of admirable behavior. . . . Of right and wrong. . . . It's heavily influenced by film.
>
> It's the most vivid and valuable record of who we were and what we were, and what we thought and what we believed. And it continues to be that.

Movies not only influenced the average moviegoer, they also inspired future filmmakers. Director Francis Ford Coppola explains how he was affected by the power of film to communicate ideas and create beauty.

> When I was about sixteen or seventeen, I began to see some of . . . the great foreign films that were being imported and were first being shown in art houses in Long Island, where they served coffee rather than Good-N-Plenty. . . .
>
> There was a tremendous, almost magnetic, response to wish that I could do it. Upon seeing a beautiful film like Fellini's *La Strada* or *The White Sheik* . . . I was just excited. If I could only go out and *do* something like this. . . .
>
> One of the many positive effects of participating in a work of art is the inspiration to want to go out and do it—even to copy it. It is a very legitimate instinct of young people—to want to imitate the things they love.

The movies also reflected our cultural norms. As Jean Firstenberg, director of the American Film Institute, expressed it, "The American motion picture is probably more representative of this country than anything else we have done creatively."

The history of American film is also the history of an art form. And, as with any

Sydney Pollack, an organizer of The Film Foundation, is seen here directing *Havana*, which starred another Film Foundation board member, Robert Redford.
Photo: Courtesy, MCA Publishing Rights, a Division of MCA Inc. Copyright © 1990 Universal City Studios, Inc.

art form, the "great works" of the "great masters" provide education and inspiration for future artists. Without these, tomorrow's filmmakers are denied their roots. Each new generation of filmmakers *needs* the cinematic works of the past, from the sublime to the ridiculous, as springboards for new directions.

At the ridiculous end of the spectrum Steven Spielberg's animated television shows *Tiny Toons* and *Animaniacs* build directly on movies of the past. Their particular past was created by Warner Bros. Animation Department during the 1940s and 1950s. Without Looney Tunes there could be no Tiny Toons. Without the inspiration of Bugs Bunny and Daffy Duck there could be no Buster Bunny and no Plucky Duck. Without the famous Warner water tower, there would be no home for the Warner brothers, Animaniacs Yakko and Wacko, and their sister Dot.

French filmmaker and critic François Truffaut became a director because of his love for the American films he saw as a boy. In his book, *The Films in My Life,* he writes passionately about the films that shaped him as an artist and as a man.

> I felt a tremendous need to enter *into* the films. I sat closer and closer to the screen so I could shut out the theater. I passed up period films, war movies, and Westerns because they were more difficult to identify with. That left mysteries and love stories. Unlike most moviegoers my own age, I didn't identify with the heroes, but with the underdog and, in general, with any character who was in the wrong. That's why Alfred Hitchcock's movies, devoted to fear, won me over from the start.

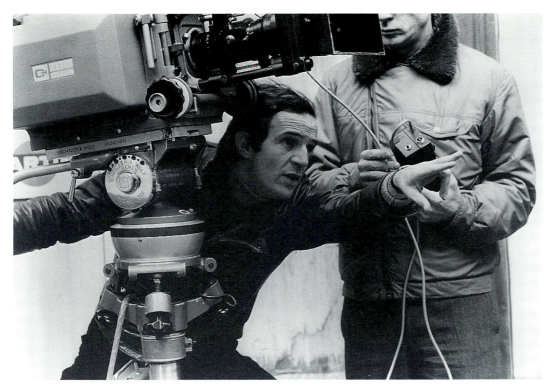

Warren Beatty commented on director François Truffaut's role as a *cinéaste:* "He was a studious and industrious film critic. He worked hard; he really looked at people's films; he loved them."
Photo: The Museum of Modern Art/Film Stills Archive.

Truffaut's work would not have been the same if he had never seen the films of Alfred Hitchcock and Charlie Chaplin or been mesmerized by Orson Welles's *Citizen Kane* (1941). Indeed, Truffaut might never have made movies at all had he not been inspired by great films.

In his autobiographical film *Day for Night* (1973), Truffaut includes dream sequences in which a small boy steals still photos of *Citizen Kane* from the local movie theater. Haunted by his affection and admiration for Orson Welles's masterpiece, Truffaut lets his audience know that his filmic images are stolen ones.

Drawing his inspiration from movies of the past, François Truffaut made films that are considered masterpieces and he has in turn become the inspiration for the next generation. Without Truffaut's *Jules et Jim* (1961), director Paul Mazursky would never have made *Willy and Phil* (1980). Now, if the works of Paul Mazursky survive the twentieth century intact, perhaps the next generation will be equally inspired and will borrow their images from him.

Woody Allen is perhaps the best-known example of a cinephile-turned-filmmaker. Allen's admiration for Humphrey Bogart and *Casablanca* (1943) inspired his *Play It Again, Sam* (1972). The influence of Swedish director Ingmar Bergman is clearly seen in *A Midsummer Night's Sex Comedy* (1982) and *Interiors* (1978). And without the inspiration of Federico Fellini's masterpiece, *8 1/2* (1963), Woody Allen's *Stardust Memories* (1980) would have looked very different . . . and might not have existed at all.

In Eric Lax's *Woody Allen: A Biography,* Allen talks nostalgically about his misspent youth—at the movies:

> I grew up at a time when . . . your basic movie was Fred Astaire or Humphrey Bogart. All those wonderful larger-than-life people. . . .
>
> This was such a glamorous time, as portrayed in films, and so great a contrast to life outside. My memory of it lingers: three hours of relentless sugar

intake; of big apartments and white phones and characters whose biggest concern was 'Who are you going to take to the Easter parade?' You were transported to Arabia, and to Paris in the 1700s, but best of all to Manhattan, which was full of gangsters and showgirls. Afterward, as you walked out up the plush red carpet, the music would be playing to end the picture or to start the next one. Then the doors opened and you were back in the blazing light, amid the meat markets and trucks honking and people walking past.

The box-office hits say a great deal about what people enjoyed at a certain time. Some of the most interesting cultural barometers, however, are yesterday's cheap independent features—subculture and counterculture films—that were never mainstream popular hits. Pornography or ethnic films can reveal as much about the dominant culture as they do about the segment of society that produced them.

For instance, during the 1930s and 1940s, there were films made exclusively for African Americans and shown in theaters that catered to what *Variety* used to call "the race trade." Whether made inside or outside of Hollywood, these films reflected political and social attitudes during a specific period in our country's history. They are unique and important records.

Sepia Cinderella (1947) is one of these significant ethnic films that has survived. The review in *Variety* described the film as retaining "the Herald Pictures formula of intertwining a series of [vaudeville] and musical acts with a slight and familiar story." The review went on to say that the movie employed well-known and popular "colored performers," featuring music by Deek Watson and His Brown Dots and comedy by Leonardo and Zolo.

Entertainment films, even though they are usually fictional stories, are also historical records of America's ever-changing point of view. Studying a topic or a single story portrayed in different epochs can give a historian insights into changing attitudes and values because they are embedded in the way in which a story is told. Compare four of

Woody Allen's great love for the mystery and magic of the movies penetrates every film he directs. Allen is one of the original board members of The Film Foundation. *Photo: Copyright © Brian Hamill, Photoreporters.*

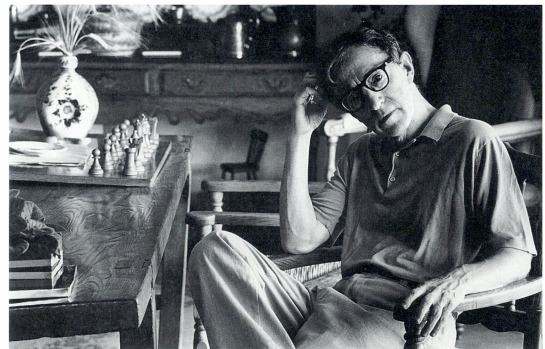

Film preservation enables us to compare versions of the same story across decades. These two versions of the Robin Hood legend say as much or more about the 1920s and 1930s in the United States as they do about twelfth-century England.

Douglas Fairbanks as Robin Hood in 1922.

Errol Flynn as Robin and Olivia de Havilland as Maid Marian with members of the Warner Bros. stock company in *The Adventures of Robin Hood* (1938).
Photo: Copyright © 1938 Turner Entertainment Co. All Rights Reserved.

the film versions of the Robin Hood legend, which are strikingly different from each other in many ways.

Robin Hood (1922), a silent film, featured the athletic and exuberant Douglas Fairbanks. In 1938 Errol Flynn was virile and romantic in *The Adventures of Robin Hood.* The 1990s brought Kevin Costner's "realistic" *Robin Hood: Prince of Thieves* and director Mel Brooks's burlesque *Robin Hood: Men in Tights.*

These films put on the screen the values of different periods in American history. They say as much or more about the 1920s, 1930s, and 1990s in the United States as they do about twelfth-century England. In each film, the art direction, the costuming, the romance with Marian, the portrayal of violence, and the treatment of political themes reveal a great deal about the time in which it was made.

I would like you also to think about the possibility that the documentary film of our time may be the entertainment film of the next century. **Real Movies**
—*Frederick Wiseman*

Entertainment films *may* be viewed as historic documents, but it is the documentaries, information films, and newsreels that are obvious historical documents intended to capture actuality. The preservation of these films is at least as vital and as urgent as the preservation of entertainment films. Newsreels make up many of the millions of feet of nitrate still waiting to be transferred to safety film, and are currently receiving top priority treatment by public archives and, in the case of Fox Movietone News, by their copyright holder.

As the motion picture newspaper, newsreels were an integral part of movie-going in America from the 1910s until the 1960s. Before the advent of television, they were, as Paramount Pictures put it, "the eyes and ears of the world."

The first newsreel company was started in Paris in 1909 by producer Charles Pathé, and by 1910 he had introduced the newsreel concept in New York City. Highly competitive newsreel companies formed in the United States, including those affiliated with the major studios such as Paramount News, M-G-M's "News of the Day," Fox Movietone News, and Pathé News, which announced each week's installment with a crowing rooster.

Newsreels covered current events from the spectacular explosion of the *Hindenburg* to presidential campaigns. Designed to entertain as well as inform, their content varied from world affairs to beauty contests to dog shows. They covered the lives of the rich and famous, whether it was Canada's Dionne quintuplets having a birthday party or the comings and goings of the Hollywood elite. They also documented the everyday and often humorous antics of "real" people. Newsreels captured the sights and sounds of American history for more than half the century and they will provide a unique record for future historians, if they survive.

Newsreels produced by Universal have survived and are preserved at the National Archives, while at the UCLA Film and Television Archive the conversion of some of the Hearst Metrotone News Collection onto safety stock is being funded by the National Endowment for the Humanities, the Joseph Drown Foundation, and the David and Lucile Packard Foundation. Concurrently, Fox Movietone News, which is still owned by Twentieth Century–Fox, is being transferred to videotape and digitally stored using computer technology.

This enormous Movietone News library includes nearly four thousand newsreels, fifty-five million feet of shorts and outtakes, and over six hundred other theatrical short subjects—a total of ten thousand hours of footage. Newsreel preservation is

Hearst Metrotone News captured the "most spectacular subject ever filmed"–the explosion of the zeppelin *Hindenburg* at Lakehurst, New Jersey, on May 6, 1937. *Photo: UCLA's Hearst Metrotone News Collection.*

a longer process than one might think; it almost always requires restoration as well. Newsreels were typically disassembled by the producers after being pulled from release. They were edited and stored as individual stories so they could be reused as "stock footage."

To transfer the entire Movietone collection to new film Fox estimated would be a ten-year project and cost at least $50 million. Instead, the studio chose to convert the

Prelude to War

- Emperor Hirohito reviews his troops at the height of Japanese military power.
- King Alexander of Yugoslavia and French foreign minister Jean Louis Barthou smile for the newsreel cameras moments before they are killed by an assassin's bullet in Marseilles, France, on October 9, 1934.

- Hitler Youth promote "Nationalism" and burn the books of noted writers in a great bonfire in May 1933.

These are a few scenes from fully restored, complete Hearst newsreels dating between 1929 and 1939 in UCLA's project "Prelude to War." With funds from the National Endowment for the Humanities, these and many other unique scenes from bike races to an interview with a mobster's "gun moll" have been transferred from nitrate to safety stock.

This grant awarded in 1993 by the NEH was the first ever given specifically for film preservation.

Photos: UCLA's Hearst Metrotone News Collection.

Emperor Hirohito.

King Alexander.

Nazi book burning.

Hitler Youth.

footage to digital information which could then be stored in computers. The program was expected to take less than eighteen months and cost closer to $5 million.

The scanner used to do the work is declassified military equipment, and the conversion of the Fox Movietone collection is its first commercial application. A computer chip made by Eastman Kodak is attached to a tiny camera lens, which scans the film and converts it into language a computer can store.

Frederick Wiseman is one of the preeminent documentarians of the twentieth century. His documentaries *High School* (1968) and *Hospital* (1970) are listed on the National Film Registry, and his films are collected by the Library of Congress and George Eastman House. He is one of the few documentarians who has seen some income from his work.

As an independent filmmaker Wiseman must face the financial burden for the preservation of his own films. The following is an excerpt from the testimony he gave at the Library of Congress's Washington, D.C., hearing on the current state of American film preservation held on February 26, 1993. Wiseman speaks not only for himself, but for all independent nonfiction filmmakers.

Frederick Wiseman's documentary *High School* (1968) is an excellent example of *cinéma vérité*, the documentary style that attempts to capture life as it is with minimal interference from the filmmaker. *High School* and *Hospital* (1970) are among a series of films Wiseman made about American social institutions. *Photo: The Museum of Modern Art/Film Stills Archive. Courtesy, Frederick Wiseman and Zipporah Films, Inc. Copyright © 1968 Zipporah Films, Inc.*

I would like you to imagine yourselves historians of twentieth-century America working in the year 2093. You would have access to the usual historical records, books, newspapers, memoranda, computer disks, still photographs, Hollywood movies, but probably not documentary films because they would not be available. Yet much of the material historians of our time will be most interested in exists in and on documentary film.

One can put aside the politics or point of view of documentary films and just look at what is shown as a form of natural history. Documentary films show how people talk, walk, dress, relate to each other, the nature of work, the social organization of society, family relations, the handling of deviant behavior, the operation of courts, the role of police, medical practices, the relationship between men and women, racial issues, the functioning of government agencies, scientific experimentation, the nature of entertainment and our music and the way it was performed. The list is obviously endless. . . .

The emphasis today is on the preservation of Hollywood movies to the almost total exclusion of documentary film material. . . .

Over the last twenty-six years, I have made twenty-six films covering a wide variety of topics drawn from the common experience of everyday life. . . . This represents about 4 million feet of negative and 4 million feet of quarter-inch tape. There is also 4 million feet of work print and 4 million feet of magnetic track. In addition, I have the original negative, interpositive, and duplicate negatives for each of the films. This represents another half million feet of film and optical track.

The cost of storing this material is about $7,000 a year. I cannot afford to continue to pay this. I am obviously going to keep all the preprint negative material but I am now forced to consider destroying the rest which consists of most of the material. Yet the kind of documentation that exists in the outtakes of films may be of most interest to historians and the general public in succeeding centuries in their efforts to reconstruct, know and understand the way we live now. . . .

I would urge you to support an archival effort that makes a systematic and enduring effort to preserve and collect documentary film material. I believe that in doing so you would make an important contribution to the future study and understanding of our times and establish a precedent that would be admired and followed.

Perhaps the most convincing reason to preserve films is the pleasure they bring us.

Many films transcend the time in which they were made and continue to move audiences generation after generation. Like music, like painting, like any other art form, these films are works of beauty to be experienced, to be cherished, and to be passed on to our children and our grandchildren.

"These images go into your mind and soul," says actress Shelley Winters. They also go into our hearts.

No matter how old a movie is, it can have the power to make us laugh and cry. Movies can take us places we've never been—to the Algerian Casbah with Pépé Le Moko or to outer space with "Hal," the on-board computer. Movies can plant new ideas, show us ourselves in ways we never dreamed possible . . . and inspire us to change.

In 1988 the UCLA Film and Television Archive launched its first Annual Festival of Preservation. Each year, the archive's director, Robert Rosen, reiterates the urgency and importance of saving America's movie heritage—what he calls "this century's collective memory."

The men and women who work diligently to save film are the most eloquent when it comes to their motivations for preserving our past in moving pictures. For Robert Rosen preserving movies is an endeavor with multiple rewards.

> . . . the joy of rescuing, just in time, a feature film from the beginning of the sound era that had survived as a single battered work print on deteriorating nitrate film stock.
>
> . . . the intellectual exhilaration of reconstructing the integral version of a classic that had been available only in bowdlerized, incomplete copies.
>
> . . . the sense of satisfaction that resulted from being able to present films as they were originally intended to be shown and the pleasure of sharing an audience's excitement at discovering a forgotten gem.

CHAPTER 2

The Library of Congress:
America's First Film Archive

Since the Library has done considerably more than half the film preservation that has actually been done, I can say it's been done by the public. The public has a great reason to take pride in film preservation. The American people have devoted more than any nation in the world to this, largely through the Library of Congress.
—*Dr. James Billington, Librarian of Congress*

As the nation's repository for copyrighted material, the Library of Congress became America's first film archive. The first motion pictures were referred to as "Edison Kinetoscopic Records" and were submitted for copyright at the Library of Congress on October 6, 1893, by W.K.L. Dickson, Thomas Edison's assistant. Ironically, the Library lost the materials.

Until 1912 when the Townsend Act recognized the film medium for copyright purposes, movies were deposited at the Library on paper. Following the Townsend Act, the Library processed copyright registrations within a day of the receipt of the films, and the films were then returned to the copyright holder because the Print Division of the Library of Congress, which handled "paper prints" of films, had no way to store volatile nitrate film.

Since the Library no longer collected copies of movies, the "paper prints" — useless for anything except as a copyright record—were locked away in an unused vault. Thus ended the Library's promise to become the "first" film archive . . . until 1942

NATIONAL FILM

REGISTRY

of the Library of Congress

This seal is used to identify movies listed on the National Film Registry. It may be used only with film versions that have been approved by the Library of Congress.
Photo: Courtesy, Library of Congress.

when Librarian Archibald MacLeish decided that the Library should be *actively* involved in the conservation of film. On January 28, 1943, MacLeish established the Motion Picture Collection and named Howard Walls, the discoverer of the "paper prints," as its curator.

A film acquisition program was started with funding from the Rockefeller Foundation. Under this program, the Museum of Modern Art (MoMA) made a list of suggested motion picture titles that should be retained by the Library of Congress. The selection process was completed in April 1945, and the Library acquired 603 reels of feature film footage. By October 1946, the collection had become the Motion Picture Division and had a staff of seventeen.

Since then the Motion Picture Division has had its ups and downs. Film preservation efforts began in the late 1940s. In conjunction with the Academy of Motion Picture Arts and Sciences, the Library converted the "paper prints" to 16mm film. Lack of

Silent star Mary Pickford's film collection was the Library of Congress's first major Hollywood acquisition. Librarian Archibald MacLeish was responsible for the coup, and after approaching Pickford, he circulated a memo that read: "I have cast my net towards the broad and blue Pacific, and hope to catch some very large and silver fish."

Mary Pickford in *Pollyanna* (1920).
Photo: Courtesy, Matty Kemp of Mary Pickford Company.

funding soon prevented the division from fully functioning; films could not be properly stored, much less preserved.

In 1947, with only a $12,000 budget to store film, the division was closed. With no funds available for copying nitrate to safety, the Library of Congress junked one-half of its rapidly deteriorating nitrate holdings between 1949 and 1959.

In the mid-1960s the Library's film program was reinvigorated. John Kuiper, a former film professor from Iowa State University, became head of the Library's "Motion Picture Section" and encouraged producers to deposit their films with the Library. During that decade, funds from the newly founded American Film Institute helped get the division back on its feet.

The Library of Congress has *records* on all American movies copyrighted since 1893. Its film collection is uneven between the period of the paper prints and the beginning of active acquisition of projection prints in the early 1940s. Since the 1970s, however, the Library has collected prints of virtually all U.S. feature films.

In 1993 Paul Spehr, former assistant chief at the Library of Congress and preservation pioneer, summed up the evolution of preservation at the Library.

> I have worked through half of the entire history of the film archive movement.
>
> The first span of this time was from 1935 to 1967—1967 because that is the year that the NEA program was established and a regular program of funding film restoration really began on a serious basis. It was a period of enthusiasm . . . when people who really loved film came into archives and worked with film because it had been such an important part of their life that they felt it was important to collect it, to organize it, and to somehow or other make it accessible to people.
>
> The late fifties and early sixties . . . [was] a transitional period . . . in which we were formalizing the preservation activities and were becoming more

In 1980, Paul Spehr (left) and Lewis Flacks (right) were U.S. delegates at an international meeting on film preservation. Spehr represented the Library of Congress and the Copyright Office. The recommendations presented in Paris to the 21st Session of the UNESCO General Conference succeeded in influencing international preservation standards.
Photo: Courtesy, Paul Spehr.

aggressive in acquiring materials for the collections. . . . We accomplished a great deal here in the United States because we were able to sweep in a lot of material. Of course, the Library was the great wastebasket for film collections . . . but the wastebasket often contained hidden treasures.

I think that we could characterize the last ten years as a period in which professionalism in the archives has become the standard rather than the exception. Now we have an archival community that has done its homework, and is ready to go to work.

But this is also a time of frustration because for the last ten years the resources that have supported film preservation have come to a grinding halt. . . .

[Now], we spend a good deal more time creating the kind of work that we should have been doing from the beginning.

The results are much better, but our ability to produce it has been declining at a rather rapid rate because there has not been an increase in resources.

Today, the Library of Congress is a central force in America's film preservation. Its Motion Picture, Broadcasting, and Recorded Sound Division, located in the Madison Build-

The Library of Congress houses one hundred million items, making it America's "largest accumulation of recorded creativity."
"Practically everything that we have, and that all other great repositories of American creativity have, is all disintegrating," says Librarian of Congress James Billington.
"The papers of the founding fathers are fine. You're dealing with vellum and parchment and high-rag-content, quality papers. . . .
"Might it be the case that film itself is not going to be the long-term preservation media of this form of American creativity?"
Photo: Courtesy, Library of Congress.

ing of the Library of Congress in Washington, D.C., is the leading publicly funded facility for the preservation of nitrate-era films. Its research collection contains more than 125,000 films, as well as television broadcasts, radio programs, and sound recordings. In 1994 the Library's holdings of nitrate preprint elements for Hollywood studios included: 3,500 Warner Bros. titles; 4,250 Columbia titles; 1,150 RKO titles; 600 Universal titles; 625 Hal Roach titles; and 200 Disney titles.

The Library of Congress is the only archive in the nation that maintains its own laboratories. Duplicating over a million feet yearly, the Library has customized equipment to handle brittle and shrunken film stock and other problems common to deteriorating nitrate. According to David Francis, the Dayton, Ohio, laboratory "is as well equipped as any other film preservation laboratory in the world."

SAVED: *Within Our Gates*

Within Our Gates (1919) is the earliest surviving feature film directed by an African American. Oscar Micheaux (1884–1951), the grandson of a slave who produced, wrote, and directed the film, was a novelist as well as the director of approximately forty-five feature films.

Within Our Gates was Micheaux's second film, following his autobiographical *The Homesteader,* made the previous year. Both in content and style *Within Our Gates* may be seen as a response to *The*

Birth of a Nation (1915), D. W. Griffith's masterly but racist landmark film.

Within Our Gates was a "lost" American film until 1989 when Susan Dalton at the National Center for Film and Video Preservation at the American Film Institute acquired a Spanish-release print entitled *La Negra.* The Spanish intertitles were not a direct translation of Micheaux's script, as could be ascertained from some English title frames that had been inadvertently left in the film.

In the new English titles every attempt was made to approximate the style and flavor of Micheaux's writing. His words were painstakingly re-created from his novels and existing film titles from his surviving film *Body and Soul* (1925).

This new version of *Within Our Gates,* now preserved on safety film at the Library of Congress, is available for the first time in seventy-five years in the Library's Video Collection.

The lynching scenes in *Within Our Gates* (1919) were censored in the United States. Many of the American films from the 1910s survived through the efforts of foreign film archives, which saved internationally distributed prints long ago abandoned or forgotten by their U.S. producers.
Photo: Courtesy, Library of Congress.

At present the Library's first preservation priority is still to copy nitrate to safety and to save so-called "orphan" films—movies that are not copyrighted by major film production companies. Among these are films produced by African Americans, ethnographic films, and Yiddish-language films. Beginning in 1989, the Library was also given responsibility for managing the daily operations of the National Film Preservation Board.

The National Film Preservation Act

I would rather watch the scene where Fredric March returns to his family [in *The Best Years of Our Lives*] than a roomful of Renoirs.

—*Representative Robert J. Mrazek*

In 1988 Congress passed the National Film Preservation Act. Sponsored by Congressman Robert Mrazek, the bill was designed to create a national film commission, complete with a film preservation board.

Additionally, the bill created the National Film Registry, requiring the Librarian of Congress to select annually twenty-five American films to be preserved in their original release version by the Library.

These films are to be of particular cultural, historical, and/or aesthetic significance. They are to be a diverse representation of American feature films—not merely a list of America's most popular films. They are to be treated as national treasures. It was Librarian James Billington's intention that these films "should suggest to the American public the breadth of great American filmmaking." Billington, the ultimate authority for the selection, is himself a "movie buff." He took care to point out that his method of selection is "a complex process . . . not an arbitrary indulgence of taste."

Films considered for the Registry must be at least ten years old, and recommendations are made annually by the National Film Preservation Board and the Library's motion picture curators and other staff members. The public is invited to make suggestions, although the annual list is not necessarily one that will appeal to the average film buff.

After sifting through hundreds of suggestions, it is finally the Librarian who names the twenty-five films. Once the titles are chosen, the Library requests that the copyright holder provide the Library with both preprint and print elements. In its bill Congress allocated up to $250,000 annually for all the activities of the National Film Preservation Board, which includes the special handling of the films.

The act was, in part, a response to the rapidly escalating concern on the part of many film artists and aficionados about copyright holders altering the original work. In particular, the computerized process of changing a black-and-white film to a color one, frequently called "colorization" or more recently "color enhancement," was an issue, but so were other techniques used in creating video releases. Many important and popular films were being materially altered to fit the television screen through the use of various techniques such as "panning and scanning," "time-compressing and expanding" or just old-fashioned editing.

The act addressed these concerns, at least as far as the Registry list was concerned. Films included on it were to be preserved in their original form *and*, if they were released on video in an altered way, were to be labeled as altered.

The act also created the National Film Preservation Board. Originally a thirteen-person advisory group, in 1992 legislation expanded this to an eighteen-member group made up of representatives from the motion picture industry, universities, film associations, and archives:

The thirteenth librarian of Congress, Dr. James H. Billington, is a self-proclaimed "movie buff." *Photo: Courtesy, Library of Congress.*

Academy of Motion Picture Arts and Sciences

Alliance of Motion Picture and Television Producers

American Film Institute

American Society of Cinematographers and the International Photographers Guild

Directors Guild of America

U.S. members of the International Federation of Film Archives

Motion Picture Association of America

National Association of Broadcasters

National Association of Theater Owners

National Society of Film Critics

Department of Film and Television of the Tisch School of the Arts at New York University

Screen Actors Guild

Society for Cinema Studies

University Film and Video Association

Department of Theater, Film, and Television of the College of Fine Arts, University of California at Los Angeles

Writers Guild of America

When the first twenty-five films on the Registry were announced in June 1989, there were some dissenting voices. Jack Valenti, a member of the Film Preservation Board and president of the Motion Picture Association of America, disapproved of the Registry

Fay Kanin, chair of the National Film Preservation Board, has been a long-time advocate for film preservation. In 1983 Kanin stated, "All art forms are buffeted by time, but ours has proved unexpectedly ephemeral. Museums can show us sculpture from 1,500 years ago and beautifully preserved books and paintings from before the fifteenth century. But most of the movies made before 1920 have already been lost to us. The roster of once-admired, now-lost pictures—including the Oscar-winning *The Patriot*—makes uneasy reading." Photo: Courtesy, Fay Kanin.

concept. "I've worked my entire career to stop governments from being involved [in the film industry], and I'm not going to vote."

Robert Rosen, also on the Preservation Board, qualified his support of the idea of a national registry. "The selection of these films serves no purpose, unless the larger issues of saving our national film heritage in its original form are addressed. . . . I'm concerned that people will feel that the saving of a handful of films will satisfy their responsibility to save their culture." Rosen added, "If this remains solely the naming of the twenty-five best films of all time, it's been a horrible waste of time." Ultimately, Rosen felt that the Registry is "a superb gesture to raise consciousness, but it doesn't save film."

Dissent also came from Samuel Goldwyn, Jr., whose father produced *The Best Years of Our Lives* (1946). Goldwyn announced he was unwilling to donate an archival quality print of the film to the Library. Goldwyn, chairman of the Samuel Goldwyn Co., said that since there was no legal obligation to give a print, he would "refrain."

He pointed out that a print had been deposited in the Library in 1946 for copyright purposes. "I see no reason to send out another copy of a film that is currently available to scholars in a number of places," Goldwyn said. "What you have here is people

"Film is part of our heritage. It is more important than the printed word. It is our history. It's knowledge. It's vital." —*David Francis, chief of the Motion Picture Division, Library of Congress*
Photo: Courtesy, David Francis. Reprinted by kind permission of the Library of Congress Gazette.

in Washington telling us that our prints are in disrepair, and that we—who spend our professional lives looking after classic film prints—are doing a substandard job of maintaining them." Goldwyn also stated that the Library can "exploit" the print with screenings, implying that they could take revenue away from the Samuel Goldwyn Co.

Some critics and journalists felt that the list was virtually a "best films of all time" list, containing titles like *Casablanca* (1943) and *Singin' in the Rain* (1952), which are so obviously of lasting value that they need no special treatment. Turner Entertainment, the copyright holder of both of these titles, would not let them deteriorate or disappear because they have too much market value.

Buster Keaton's comic genius reached its zenith with *The General* (1927), a brilliant blending of action, romance, and comedy. "I realized," said Keaton, "that my feature comedies would succeed best when the audience took the plot seriously enough to root for me as I worked my way out of mounting perils."

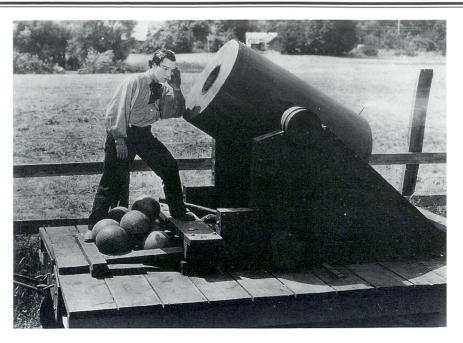

The National Film Registry: 1989

The Best Years of Our Lives (1946)

Casablanca (1943)

Citizen Kane (1941)

The Crowd (1928)

Dr. Strangelove; or, How I Learned to Stop Worrying and Love the Bomb (1964)

The General (1927)

Gone With the Wind (1939)

The Grapes of Wrath (1940)

High Noon (1952)

Intolerance (1916)

The Learning Tree (1969)

The Maltese Falcon (1941)

Mr. Smith Goes to Washington (1939)

Modern Times (1936)

Nanook of the North (1921)

On the Waterfront (1954)

The Searchers (1956)

Singin' in the Rain (1952)

Snow White and the Seven Dwarfs (1937)

Some Like It Hot (1959)

Star Wars (1977)

Sunrise (1927)

Sunset Boulevard (1950)

Vertigo (1958)

The Wizard of Oz (1939)

All About Eve (1950), a sophisticated and cynical look at backstage theater life, was a highly acclaimed box-office success. Nominated for an impressive fourteen Academy Awards, it won six, including Best Picture. Joseph Mankiewicz's literate and satiric script furnishes great lines and memorable scenes for a brilliant ensemble cast which includes, left to right, Bette Davis, Gary Merrill, Anne Baxter, and George Sanders.
Photo: Courtesy of Twentieth Century–Fox and the Estate of Bette Davis. Copyright © 1950 Twentieth Century–Fox Film Corporation. All Rights Reserved.

The National Film Registry: 1990

All About Eve (1950)

All Quiet on the Western Front (1930)

Bringing Up Baby (1938)

Dodsworth (1936)

Duck Soup (1933)

Fantasia (1940)

The Freshman (1925)

The Godfather (1972)

The Great Train Robbery (1903)

Harlan County, U.S.A. (1976)

How Green Was My Valley (1941)

It's a Wonderful Life (1946)

Killer of Sheep (1977)

Love Me Tonight (1932)

Meshes of the Afternoon (1943)

Ninotchka (1939)

Primary (1960)

Raging Bull (1980)

Rebel Without a Cause (1955)

Red River (1948)

The River (1937)

Sullivan's Travels (1941)

Top Hat (1935)

The Treasure of the Sierra Madre (1948)

A Woman Under the Influence (1974)

A landmark film in animation, *Gertie the Dinosaur* (1914), was produced by cartoonist Winsor McCay. McCay (who created the comic strip *Little Nemo*) made 10,000 ink drawings of Gertie on rice paper. The film is *fully animated*—one new drawing for each frame of film—and truly began the art of character animation, showing personality through movement. *Gertie* was originally made for McCay's vaudeville act, in which the artist talked to Gertie, who was projected on a screen. When the film went into distribution as a one-reeler, McCay combined the animated Gertie with a live-action story.

The National Film Registry: 1991

The Battle of San Pietro (1945)

The Blood of Jesus (1941)

Chinatown (1974)

City Lights (1931)

David Holzman's Diary (1968)

Frankenstein (1931)

Gertie the Dinosaur (1914)

Gigi (1958)

Greed (1924)

High School (1968)

I Am a Fugitive from a Chain Gang (1932)

The Italian (1915)

King Kong (1933)

Lawrence of Arabia (1962)

The Magnificent Ambersons (1942)

My Darling Clementine (1946)

Out of the Past (1947)

A Place in the Sun (1951)

The Poor Little Rich Girl (1917)

The Prisoner of Zenda (1937)

Shadow of a Doubt (1943)

Sherlock, Jr. (1924)

Tevya (1939)

Trouble in Paradise (1932)

2001: A Space Odyssey (1968)

Salt of the Earth (1954) was written by Academy Award winner Michael Wilson, directed by Herbert Biberman, one of "The Hollywood Ten," and produced by Academy Award nominee Paul Jarrico. All three were on the Hollywood blacklist at the time.

The story of a strike by zinc miners in New Mexico, *Salt of the Earth* was filmed in a "documentary" style using nonprofessional actors. Actual participants in the strike play roles in the movie.

The film caused a political furor. Union projectionists refused to screen it and no major distributor would release it. The French, however, honored it with the International Grand Prix for best picture shown in France in 1955.
Photo: The Museum of Modern Art/Film Stills Archive. Courtesy, Paul Jarrico.

The National Film Registry: 1992

Adam's Rib (1949)
Annie Hall (1977)
The Bank Dick (1940)
Big Business (1929)
The Big Parade (1925)
The Birth of a Nation (1915)
Bonnie and Clyde (1967)
Carmen Jones (1954)
Castro Street (1966)
Detour (1945)
Dog Star Man (1964)
Double Indemnity (1944)
Footlight Parade (1933)
The Gold Rush (1925)
Letter from an Unknown Woman (1948)
Morocco (1930)
Nashville (1975)
The Night of the Hunter (1955)
Paths of Glory (1957)
Psycho (1960)
Ride the High Country (1962)
Salesman (1969)
Salt of the Earth (1954)
What's Opera, Doc? (1957)
Within Our Gates (1919)

Stars Cary Grant and Rosalind Russell shine in *His Girl Friday* (1940), the Howard Hawks–directed screwball comedy that has been restored by the UCLA Film and Television Archive to its original fast-paced, wisecracking brilliance.

His Girl Friday is a reworking of Ben Hecht and Charles MacArthur's hit play *The Front Page,* in which Walter Burns and Hildy Johnson were men. By making "Hildy" the diminutive of "Hildegarde" and casting Russell opposite Grant, Hawks added the delightful twist of romantic attraction and tension between editor and reporter.

Photo: Courtesy, Columbia Pictures. Copyright © 1939 Columbia Pictures Corp. All Rights Reserved.

The National Film Registry: 1993

An American in Paris (1951)

Badlands (1973)

The Black Pirate (1926)

Blade Runner (1982)

Cat People (1942)

The Cheat (1915)

Chulas Fronteras (1976)

Eaux d'Artifice (1953)

The Godfather, Part II (1974)

His Girl Friday (1940)

It Happened One Night (1934)

Lassie Come Home (1943)

Magical Maestro (1952)

March of Time: Inside Nazi Germany (1938)

A Night at the Opera (1935)

Nothing But a Man (1964)

One Flew Over the Cuckoo's Nest (1975)

Point of Order (1964)

Shadows (1959)

Shane (1953)

Sweet Smell of Success (1957)

Touch of Evil (1958)

Where Are My Children? (1916)

The Wind (1928)

Yankee Doodle Dandy (1942)

Silent film comedian Harold Lloyd hangs in peril in one of his famous features, *Safety Last* (1923). Scenes like this, the result of eye-tricking set construction and careful camera placement, had audiences gasping at their derring-do.
Photo: Courtesy, The Harold Lloyd Trust/First Interstate Bank.

The National Film Registry: 1994

The African Queen (1951)

The Apartment (1960)

The Cool World (1963)

A Corner in Wheat (1909)

E.T. The Extra-Terrestrial (1982)

The Exploits of Elaine (1914)

Force of Evil (1948)

Freaks (1932)

Hell's Hinges (1916)

Hospital (1970)

Invasion of the Body Snatchers (1956)

The Lady Eve (1941)

Louisiana Story (1948)

The Manchurian Candidate (1962)

Marty (1955)

Meet Me in St. Louis (1944)

Midnight Cowboy (1969)

A Movie (1958)

Pinocchio (1940)

Safety Last (1923)

Scarface (1932)

Snow White (1933)

Tabu (1931)

Taxi Driver (1976)

Zapruder Film (1963)

The Last of the Mohicans (1920) has been restored by George Eastman House. This majestic silent version of James Fenimore Cooper's classic story set during the French and Indian War was directed by Maurice Tourneur and Clarence Brown. The restored version was one of the features aired in AMC's first annual Film Preservation Festival. *Photo: Courtesy, George Eastman House.*

The National Film Registry: 1995

The Adventures of Robin Hood (1938)

All That Heaven Allows (1955)

American Graffiti (1973)

The Band Wagon (1953)

Blacksmith Scene (1893)

Cabaret (1972)

Chan Is Missing (1982)

The Conversation (1974)

The Day the Earth Stood Still (1951)

El Norte (1983)

Fatty's Tintype Tangle (1915)

The Four Horsemen of the Apocalypse (1921)

Fury (1936)

Gerald McBoing Boing (1951)

The Hospital (1971)

Jammin' the Blues (1944)

The Last of the Mohicans (1920)

Manhatta (1921)

North by Northwest (1959)

The Philadelphia Story (1940)

Rip Van Winkle (1896)

Seventh Heaven (1927)

Stagecoach (1939)

To Fly (1976)

To Kill a Mockingbird (1962)

Lillian Gish, shown here in *Broken Blossoms* (1919), contributed greatly to the art of silent movies and was a good friend to film preservation. Miss Gish addressed a congressional subcommittee in 1979 to plead for the preservation of newsreels, which she described as the living record of America's powerful history. *Broken Blossoms* is one of many D. W. Griffith masterpieces safeguarded by the Museum of Modern Art in New York City.

Photo: Copyright © 1996 The Museum of Modern Art, New York.

The National Film Registry: 1996

The Awful Truth (1937)
Broken Blossoms (1919)
The Deer Hunter (1978)
Destry Rides Again (1939)
Flash Gordon (1936)
The Forgotten Frontier (1931)
Frank Film (1973)
The Graduate (1967)
The Heiress (1949)
The Jazz Singer (1927)
The Life and Times of Rosie the Riveter (1980)
*M*A*S*H* (1970)
Mildred Pierce (1945)

The Outlaw Josey Wales (1976)
The Producers (1968)
Pull My Daisy (1959)
Road to Morocco (1942)
She Done Him Wrong (1933)
Shock Corridor (1963)
Show Boat (1936)
The Thief of Bagdad (1924)
To Be or Not to Be (1942)
Topaz (1943–1945)
Verbena Tragica (1939)
Woodstock (1970)

Turner Entertainment is the copyright holder of seven of the first twenty-five titles to be named to the National Film Registry. They include one of America's best-loved movies, *Casablanca* (1943), which artfully blends a story of romance, intrigue, and noble sacrifice, and speaks as strongly to audiences today as it did to moviegoers during World War II. A superb example of wartime studio product, it was also a critical success and was nominated for eight Oscars, winning Best Picture, Best Director, and Best Screenplay for 1943. Here Humphrey Bogart, Claude Rains, Paul Henreid, and Ingrid Bergman meet in Rick's Café Americain.
Photo: Copyright © 1943 Turner Entertainment Co. All Rights Reserved.

This would seem an obvious point, yet it was not the case with at least one of the first twenty-five films named to the Registry, *Vertigo* (1958). While under the care of copyright holder Alfred Hitchcock Productions, the film's original camera negative and other materials vital to its preservation seriously deteriorated. In May 1993 the *Los Angeles Times* reported that the Eastman Color negative for Hitchcock's suspense film was fading fast and that director Martin Scorsese had personally approached Universal Pictures chairman Tom Pollock about the need to restore it.

For the independently produced *Vertigo,* some delays in preservation had arisen because no one owned the film outright. Universal Pictures holds some rights, but it belongs essentially to Hitchcock's estate, controlled by his daughter, Patricia. With both Universal and the Hitchcock estate holding rights to *Vertigo,* its proper preservation was delayed—almost too long to save the film.

According to independent preservation expert Robert Harris, when he began work on the restoration he found the original negative was in a near total state of deterioration. "The negative was so bad that there was no way you could strike a good print," Harris told *Daily Variety*. "It's an important film, and it needed to be done," Harris said. "If somebody didn't do something about it now, it would be a lost film. We couldn't find one good print from 1958. The L.A. Conservancy showed one in downtown L.A. to a packed house [in 1995], and the best print they could get was awful."

Harris, and his partner Jim Katz, premiered their restoration of *Vertigo* in October 1996 at the New York Film Festival, following two years of painstaking work. Thanks to their dedication, another important wide-screen title has been saved.

In 1990 the second set of twenty-five films was selected from among 1,465 nominations made by the public and those made by the Preservation Board. Again, most of the films on the list were acknowledged classics. According to Library of Congress curator Patrick Loughney, about 60 percent of the 1990 selections had won some type of Academy Award, while 80 percent had won other major awards.

The list also represented a broader range of non-Hollywood product including the documentaries *Primary* (1960) and *Harlan County, U.S.A.* (1976), the independent feature *Killer of Sheep* (1977), and an "art film," *Meshes of the Afternoon* (1943). And despite the attitude of Samuel Goldwyn, Jr., the Librarian named another Goldwyn classic, *Dodsworth* (1936), to the 1990 list.

By the time the 1991 list was announced, thirty-eight of the first fifty copyright holders had sent or promised to send material. The next twenty-five titles were the most diverse to date, and the first seventy-five titles now included silent films, musicals, cartoons, *films noir*, minority films, plain stock-in-trade whodunits, Westerns, and avant-garde films. The Registry even listed a religious allegory originally made for African-American audiences, *The Blood of Jesus* (1941).

As was the case with *Vertigo*, one of the best-known films on the 1991 list had already faced serious preservation problems. The nitrate negative for *A Place in the Sun* (1951), directed by George Stevens, had already "self-destructed." This does not mean the film is lost, however. "We have three pages' worth of computer inventory on all of the safety internegatives that we have on that title," says Philip E. Murphy, a vice president at Paramount, the film's copyright holder. "The Library will be receiving a pristine print struck from one of those negatives."

In 1992 the National Film Preservation Act was reauthorized, extending the National Film Preservation Board and the Registry for four more years. Funds were allocated at $250,000 each year, and the Library was directed to conduct a study on the current state of film preservation in the United States. Following the completion of the study, the Library would make recommendations to Congress for a national preservation plan.

Meshes of the Afternoon (1943), the influential experimental film by Maya Deren, was named in 1990 to the National Film Registry. In 1946, Deren wrote: "Cinema . . . is a time-space art with a unique capacity for creating new temporal-spatial relationships and projecting them with an incontrovertible impact of reality—the reality of show-it-to-me." *Photo: The Museum of Modern Art/Film Stills Archive.*

Vaudeville and the New York stage were training grounds for many outstanding film personalities. These variety artists served a rugged apprenticeship and honed their skills in front of every kind of audience. W. C. Fields was a star in vaudeville before he was twenty. A man of remarkable dexterity, Fields's juggling skills can still be appreciated in his features and shorts.

Shemp Howard, one of the original Three Stooges, perfected his talents in vaudeville and the New York theater, as did The Marx Brothers.

Many Broadway plays and vaudeville acts were recorded faithfully on film, making such movies our only remaining visual record of popular live performances of the first half of the twentieth century. Both *The Bank Dick* and *Duck Soup* have been chosen for the National Film Registry, preserving stage as well as screen art for future generations.

W. C. Fields questions Shemp Howard as Russell Hicks prepares to join the conversation in *The Bank Dick* (1940).
Photo: Courtesy, MCA Publishing Rights, a Division of MCA Inc. Copyright © Universal City Studios, Inc.

Rufus T. Firefly casts amorous eyes on wealthy widow Gloria Teasdale. Margaret Dumont with Groucho Marx in *Duck Soup* (1933).
Photo: Courtesy, MCA Publishing Rights, a Division of MCA Inc. Copyright © Universal City Studios, Inc.

Again there was disappointment with Congress's decision, particularly from the Directors Guild of America, because the new bill eliminated the "labeling law," which required "ancillary exhibitors" to label a film that had been electronically altered. Others were pleased with inclusion of a Warner Bros. cartoon, *What's Opera, Doc?* (1957), and a "B-picture," Edgar Ulmer's *Detour* (1945), among the 1992 entries.

In 1993, 1994, 1995, and 1996 the Library added another one hundred films to the National Registry and completed a two-part report to Congress on the current state of film preservation in the United States. Published in 1993 in four volumes, the report revealed the enormous problems facing film preservation. In August 1994, this was followed by a second publication, which proposed a national plan for film preservation. In the fall of 1996, the National Film Preservation Act once again faced renewal.

In October 1996, President Bill Clinton signed the National Film Preservation Act of 1996, which not only reauthorized the National Film Preservation Act for seven additional years but also created the ground-breaking National Film Preservation Foundation.

"The annual selection of films to the National Film Registry involves much more than the simple naming of cherished and important films to a prestigious list," explained

Librarian of Congress James H. Billington when he announced the 1996 titles. "This process serves as an invaluable means to advance public awareness of the richness and variety of the American film heritage, and to dramatize the need for preservation. . . .

"The selection of a film, I stress, is not an endorsement of its ideology or content, but rather a recognition of the film's importance for America's film and cultural history. I hope the American public will note these twenty-five films, appreciate the artistry involved, and comprehend the importance of protecting these films and the rest of America's endangered film heritage."

Iris Barry's Legacy

Unless something is done to restore and preserve outstanding films of the past and the present, the motion picture from 1894 will be as irrevocably lost as the commedia dell'arte or the dancing of Nijinsky.

—*Iris Barry, first curator, Museum of Modern Art Film Library*

Today in the United States, in addition to the Library of Congress, there are three large, publicly funded archives involved in film preservation. These are the Museum of Modern Art, George Eastman House, and the UCLA Film and Television Archive. Together with the Library of Congress (which holds most of the films collected by the American Film Institute), they house more than 224,000 film titles, which far exceeds the number held by the motion picture studios.

When combined with the National Archives' collection of government films, these institutions are responsible for about 89 percent of the total film footage held by public institutions. Here resides the largest share of the remaining nitrate collections, while the studios have most of the post-1950 elements.

Together, these four archives hold a balanced portfolio of endangered, pre-1950 American movies. Together, they are working to solve the overwhelming problem of how to save them.

The Museum of Modern Art:
Where Preservation Began

My point has always been . . . we are stable. We are poor. We're desperately poor. But we *are* stable. The Library of Congress, MoMA, and Eastman House will be there long after businesses have come and gone, long after we've come and gone.

—*Mary Lea Bandy, chief curator, Museum of Modern Art Film Library*

In May of 1935, the Museum of Modern Art established its Film Library with John Abbott as director. Its creation marked the inception of film preservation in America. The library's first curator was Iris Barry, Abbott's wife. During her tenure, from 1935 to 1951, Iris Barry searched the world for film and saved thousands of motion pictures.

The Museum of Modern Art was founded in 1929 and its multi-department concept, borrowed from Germany's Bauhaus Museum, included the commercial and

popular arts as well as the fine arts. Alfred Barr, MoMA's first director, was eager to include the popular art of film in the museum setting. In 1932 he wrote, "People who are well acquainted with modern painting or literature or the theatre are amazingly ignorant of modern films."

Barr was speaking of "film as art," an idea that had flowered in Europe during the 1920s. "It may be said without exaggeration," Barr concluded, "that the only great art peculiar to the twentieth century is practically unknown to the American public most capable of appreciating it."

Formerly a film critic for *The Spectator* in London and an editor for the *Daily Mail,* British-born Iris Barry was just the person to promote film as art in the United States. Equipped with a sizable intellect and a powerful personality, Barry was "a woman of great style and wit and savoir faire," says Mary Lea Bandy. Barry saw her mission with the Film Library as first and foremost "to create a consciousness of history and tradition within the new art of the motion picture."

Her scope was international, and her goal was to assemble a film collection that illustrated the important historical and artistic steps in the development of motion pictures since their inception.

The Museum of Modern Art's Department of Film has more than thirteen thousand films, four million stills, and a growing collection of videotape.
Photo: Scott Frances/Esto. Copyright © 1994 The Museum of Modern Art, New York.

Her pioneering efforts did not go unnoticed. In 1938 MoMA received a special Oscar for collecting film and making it available for study. Forty years later, the museum received a second Academy Award specifically for increasing the public's perception of movies as an art form.

Iris Barry's original Film Library was not only designed to collect and to protect film as modern art, but also to serve as a basis for a repertory theater for public screenings of classic movies. Equally important was her educational goal: to create a circulating collection available to schools at reasonable rates. Today MoMA remains the only American archive with a circulating film library, distributing 16mm films to schools, universities, libraries, festivals, and other archives.

Daily screenings began in 1939 in the museum's 450-seat theater and continue today. The screenings became a model for archives and museums across the country, giving the public a unique opportunity to view classic and contemporary motion pictures in a museum setting.

After silent film director D. W. Griffith donated his papers, negatives, and prints to the museum, Iris Barry showcased his films in 1939. By showing the evolution of Griffith's techniques and studying his work in its original form and historical context, Barry successfully demonstrated how and why he was a pivotal film pioneer. According to Mary Lea Bandy, "What the Griffith project established was the curatorial apparatus for the medium of film."

As was the case with all these institutions, with a film collection came the burden of preservation. By 1985 MoMA's film department was the repository for eight thousand unstable nitrate-based films whose conversion to stable stock was only about half completed. Chief Curator Mary Lea Bandy estimated it would take five to ten years to complete preservation of these films—"If we have sufficient money and sufficient time in the lab."

"We want preserved films to make a profitable return to their makers. What we want most of all is to be *partners* in this effort, to serve as consultants on issues on which we have expertise: exhibition, restoration, audience development, and distribution."
—*Mary Lea Bandy*
Photo: Courtesy, The Museum of Modern Art, New York.

Those ten years have elapsed. While many of the films have been saved, MoMA's collection continues to grow. By 1994 it had expanded to more than thirteen thousand titles. As these numbers grow so do the film department's financial burdens. Films deteriorate faster than the archive can keep up. Bandy and her staff are waging a losing campaign against time. "Lack of funds," she says, is always the problem.

MoMA's most urgent goal remains the transfer of nitrate to safety stock. The museum's budget supports preservation of up to one hundred titles annually. How many films are *actually* completed depends not only on funds, but also on lab capabilities and staff availability.

"You try to do as much as you can every year within the capabilities," says Bandy. "All the labs have increased their capacity for work in the last few years. If we can raise more money, we'll expand into the preservation of independents, experimental films, color films, and films on acetate stock."

The museum's collection includes art and avant-garde films as well as Hollywood-produced movies, and boasts a noteworthy representation of important silent film-makers. These include, in addition to the valuable Griffith collection, films of superstars

Harold Lloyd was one of the first of Iris Barry's group of Hollywood producers to donate his pictures to the Museum of Modern Art in 1935. His movie *The Freshman* (1925) was added to the National Film Registry in 1990.
Photo: Courtesy, The Harold Lloyd Trust/First Interstate Bank.

Mary Pickford and Douglas Fairbanks, comedian Harold Lloyd, and Western star William S. Hart.

The museum has restored and reconstructed several of Griffith's most important titles, including *The Birth of a Nation* (1915) and *Intolerance* (1916). These "new" films have been shown around the world accompanied by the restored orchestral scores.

In 1979 the museum began the reconstruction of *Way Down East* (1920), Griffith's gripping melodrama starring silent screen greats Lillian Gish and Richard Barthelmess. *Way Down East* was Griffith's successful attempt to make a profitable film. It had been a popular stage melodrama and the director paid dearly for the literary rights.

The original version of *Way Down East* ran 150 minutes. By 1921 footage was already lost, and by 1931 the movie had been cut down to 110 minutes for sound reissue. Many of these edits were made by Griffith himself, who never gave up tinkering with his films.

When MoMA preservationist Peter Williamson set out to restore the film to its premiere length, complete with originally tinted scenes, he had as his guide the Library of Congress's complete list of shots and intertitles and the film's musical score, which accompanied the original screenings.

It took Williamson five years to piece the film together and cost the museum $70,000,

D. W. Griffith directs Richard Barthelmess, Lillian Gish, and Lowell Sherman (far right) in *Way Down East* (1920). The film was immensely successful, artistically and commercially, but was Griffith's last such success. A "soap opera" of its day, *Way Down East* is a melodrama of wronged innocence avenged, complete with a thrilling climactic pursuit across ice floes.

but the archivist succeeded in reconstructing the film at the length at which it originally premiered. Still photographs and other illustrative material from the period were used to replace lost footage.

The beautiful results were worth the price. In 1985 the restored film played to a sellout crowd at the U.S. Film Festival in Park City, Utah, and received a standing ovation.

Films are windows into the past.
    —Jan-Christopher Horak, former senior curator, George Eastman House

The George Eastman House: Celluloid in a Colonial Manse

In Rochester, New York, at the former home of George Eastman, some of America's most important films are safeguarded. Adjacent to Eastman's fabulous fifty-room Colonial Revival mansion, which was completed in 1905, is a new 73,000-square-foot, climate-controlled, postmodern wing, which was completed in 1989 and now houses the International Museum of Photography and Film.

Commonly called "George Eastman House," the museum is named for the photographic pioneer and founder of the Eastman Kodak Company. The museum was chartered in 1947 and opened its doors in 1949.

James Card, the film archive's first curator, is distinguished as the only film collector to have established an American film archive. He was aggressive about acquisition and preservation in the style of his close friend, Henri Langlois, the film champion of France.

The basis of the Eastman House collection was a group of twenty mint-condition Edison films which predated 1897; the Francis Doublier collection, which included early cameras and projectors; and, not surprisingly, James Card's personal collection. It was

The Dryden Theatre at the George Eastman House opened in 1951.
Photo: Courtesy, George Eastman House.

George Eastman, founder of the Eastman Kodak Company, lived in this Colonial Revival mansion from 1905 until his death in 1932. Its restoration was completed in 1990. At the same time, this adjoining state-of-the-art facility, the Archives Building, was constructed. It houses the museum's archives and galleries.
Photos: Barbara Puorro Galasso.
Courtesy, George Eastman House.

a humble beginning for a motion picture collection at what was essentially a museum of the history of still photography. Card himself called the film collection the museum's "country cousin."

Like Iris Barry, James Card was a visionary who saw many reasons to preserve film. Card valued film as a historical record of the major developments in motion picture technique and a document of changing social issues. He regarded newsreels and documentaries as source material that captured authentic cultural details such as dress and architecture. Card knew that the preservation of films from various epochs

A film collector who founded an archive, James Card
was aggressive about film acquisition and preservation
in the style of Henri Langlois, the film champion
of the Cinémathèque in France.
Photo: Courtesy, George Eastman House.

Dr. Jan-Christopher "Chris" Horak at George Eastman
House, where he worked for ten years, seven of them as
head of the film department. Horak is credited with
opening the film collection to filmmakers, researchers,
and media arts centers after years of inaccessibility.
He significantly expanded Eastman House's film holdings,
most notably through the acquisition of the Martin
Scorsese collection. In 1994, Dr. Horak took the
position of director of the Filmmuseum in Munich,
one of the three major film archives in Germany.
Photo: David Gibney.
Courtesy, George Eastman House.

meant that scholars could trace the careers of leading artists, and learn the history of film techniques and technology, as well as compare versions of film stories across decades.

Since 1947 Eastman House's holdings have expanded to over twenty-one thousand titles, which include twelve million feet of nitrate. Its collection of silent films contains works by pioneer Thomas H. Ince, silent film director Maurice Tourneur, actress Louise Brooks, and producer/director Cecil B. DeMille. There is a complete Greta Garbo silent collection, except for two "lost" films. It also houses the M-G-M collection, both silent and sound titles.

"Our silent film collection is one of the best parts of our collection," says the archive's former senior curator, Dr. Jan-Christopher Horak. "Our first curator, James Card, specialized in silent film simply because this was the film that no one was presumably interested in at the time."

Like the Museum of Modern Art, Eastman House has restored some important silent films. They include Lon Chaney's *Hunchback of Notre Dame* (1923), *The Crowd* (1928), which is now listed on the National Film Registry, and the spectacular *Ben Hur* (1926). The archive's preservations of *The Last of the Mohicans* (1920), directed by Maurice Tourneur and Clarence Brown, and *The Lost World* (1925) were funded in part by the National Endowment for the Arts.

Paolo Cherchi Usai, senior curator of the Motion Picture Department, has seen George Eastman House enter an important new era. In the summer of 1996 the archive opened a new storage building for its nitrate holdings, "The Louis B. Mayer Conservation Center," and that fall launched a ground-breaking school for preservationists. Both projects were supported by funding from the Louis B. Mayer Foundation.
Dr. Cherchi Usai was formerly head of Restorations Projects at the Royal Film Archive in Brussels while simultaneously teaching film studies at the University of Liège in Belgium. He had previously served as assistant curator of the film collection at George Eastman House, and in the late 1980s was deputy curator at Cineteca del Friuli, Gemona del Friuli, Italy.
Photo: Courtesy, George Eastman House.

Long before *Jurassic Park, The Lost World* (1925) thrilled audiences with ferocious dinosaurs. *The Lost World* combined live action, stop-motion animation, special effects, and a gripping adventure story. It is one of the many films preserved at George Eastman House. Willis H. O'Brien, who created the special effects, went on to become the chief technician on *King Kong* (1933).

The Lost World, along with other Eastman House–preserved titles, *The Phantom of the Opera* and *The Last of the Mohicans,* is now available on laser disk from Lumivision Corporation. Located in Denver, Colorado, Lumivision was directly involved in the restoration of *The Lost World,* particularly in the adjustment of "projection" speed when it was transferred to the digital format. This restored version includes tinted and toned scenes as well as a new, original score by R. J. Miller.

The archive has contributed to the preservation of such M-G-M classics as *Gone With the Wind* (1939) and *Meet Me in St. Louis* (1944), for which it lent Turner Entertainment the original Technicolor negatives. Eastman House's biggest "attention-getter," says Chris Horak, was its preservation of *The Phantom of the Opera* (1925). The archive managed to find color material, which was combined with original material housed at Eastman.

Eastman House also specializes in collecting classic French and German titles and post–World War II American documentaries, including the work of independent filmmakers such as Frederick Wiseman and Les Blank. It is also the repository for director Martin Scorsese's film collection, which alone contains over three thousand titles.

In addition, the archive houses paper material related to movies—three million stills, lobby cards, and ten thousand posters—as well as an outstanding collection focusing on the technological history of photography.

We have a unique collection here—unique in the country and, indeed, in the world.   —*Robert Rosen, director, UCLA Film and Television Archive*

**The UCLA Film and Television Archive:
A Nice Home for Old Films**

The youngest of America's major film archives sits closest to Hollywood at the University of California at Los Angeles. Tucked against the hills above Westwood Village is UCLA's Film and Television Archive, founded in 1965 by Colin Young, a former chairman of the university's Theatre Arts Department.

Since then the UCLA Film and Television Archive has become the largest aggregate collection in any university setting in the world and, in the United States, it is second in size only to the Library of Congress.

The archive's first important collection came from Paramount Pictures in 1970. Along with scripts and stills, the studio donated nitrate prints of approximately 740 titles produced between 1928 and 1948 to the new archive. This was followed by impressive acquisitions of nitrate prints from Twentieth Century–Fox and from Warner Bros.

From these seminal collections performances of Hollywood's greatest stars from the Golden Era are being preserved. Marlene Dietrich, Gary Cooper, Bing Crosby, and John Wayne can be seen once again in pristine prints of their classic films *Morocco* (1930), *For Whom the Bell Tolls* (1943), *Road to Rio* (1947), and *Stagecoach* (1939).

In Westwood and in the old Technicolor building in Hollywood where the actual preservation work is done, approximately forty-six thousand film titles are stored. Twenty-five million feet of this film is nitrate. In many cases, these titles are the only extant copies in the world.

Thousands of feet of this film disappear every year. "It is demoralizing to realize

One of the many movies "saved" by UCLA is *This Is the Army,* featuring George Murphy, Ronald Reagan, Joan Leslie, and Charles Butterworth. Released in 1943, the film is one of the highest-grossing American musicals of all time.
Photo: The Museum of Modern Art/Film Stills Archive.

Maurice Tourneur directed Mary Pickford in *The Poor Little Rich Girl* (1917), casting the twenty-four-year-old actress as a child. Mary went on to play a host of famous children including *Little Lord Fauntleroy*, *Rebecca of Sunnybrook Farm*, *The Little Princess*, and *Pollyanna*, cementing her title as "America's Sweetheart."
Photo: The Museum of Modern Art/Film Stills Archive. Courtesy, Matty Kemp of Mary Pickford Company.

that despite our best efforts, we are losing the race against time," says Robert Rosen, the archive's director since 1974.

One of the archive's most significant holdings is *not* feature films. It is the Hearst Metrotone News Collection, which was donated to UCLA by the Hearst Corporation in 1982 and is owned by the people of California. The collection includes newsreel coverage that dates from 1919 to 1968 and provides valuable primary documents of the people, places, and events of the twentieth century.

Nearly half of the Hearst footage was shot during the 1930s, and this is currently receiving the archive's top priority. It totals twenty-five million feet and contains eleven million feet of nitrate footage. With funds from the National Endowment for the Humanities, the archive is transferring many unique scenes from the 1930s from nitrate to safety stock.

In 1977, when Robert Gitt joined UCLA's preservation staff, the archive added restoration to its efforts. In 1984, Gitt's landmark restoration of *Becky Sharp* (1935), the first three-strip Technicolor feature, brought the archive to national prominence.

Gitt's talent and his commitment to the future of the moving image have made him one of the preeminent preservation experts in the world and one of the field's most ardent crusaders. In 1994 he explained how he viewed the future of preservation:

So often we talk about very old movies, and people could get the impression that preservation involves musty old films of the past or films of our parents' or grandparents' time.

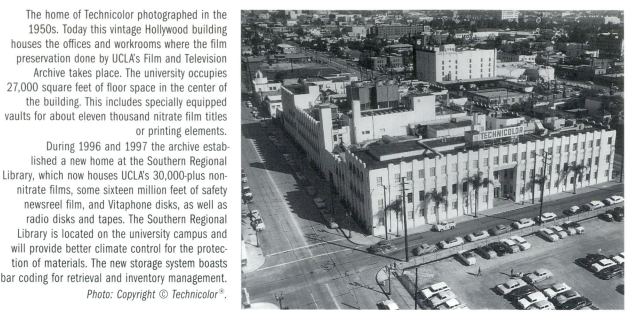

The home of Technicolor photographed in the 1950s. Today this vintage Hollywood building houses the offices and workrooms where the film preservation done by UCLA's Film and Television Archive takes place. The university occupies 27,000 square feet of floor space in the center of the building. This includes specially equipped vaults for about eleven thousand nitrate film titles or printing elements.

During 1996 and 1997 the archive established a new home at the Southern Regional Library, which now houses UCLA's 30,000-plus non-nitrate films, some sixteen million feet of safety newsreel film, and Vitaphone disks, as well as radio disks and tapes. The Southern Regional Library is located on the university campus and will provide better climate control for the protection of materials. The new storage system boasts bar coding for retrieval and inventory management.
Photo: Copyright © Technicolor®.

Actually, film preservation is an ongoing priority. It's very important that we concern ourselves, not only with the films of the past but also with the films and television programs of today. These are in danger as well.

Preservation must be concerned with the future, too—as more and more films are generated, along with television programs, and new forms of entertainment.

So, down the road, there's going to be more and more need to safeguard and preserve these moving images and sounds and make sure that they survive for the future.

Like the Museum of Modern Art, UCLA regularly screens its collection for students and for the public. The archive's on-campus theater in Melnitz Hall hosts five hundred to six hundred screenings of classic and contemporary films each year. In 1988 UCLA began annual preservation festivals that have greatly increased public awareness about film preservation and have provided the archive with an opportunity to show the beautiful and meaningful results of its efforts.

"We have managed in the past sixteen years to rescue nearly one thousand films, a million feet of newsreel, and nearly one hundred television programs from destruction," says Rosen. In addition to saving many short subjects and cartoons, the archive's 1996 preservation festival program lists over 260 films as "preserved."

Rosen, like many of his colleagues, feels strongly that it is not enough just to save a movie. Movies are saved so that they can be *seen*—seen the way they were originally meant to be seen, projected in a theater in front of an audience. Rosen believes that television programming of classic films and the videocassette market do not completely satisfy many viewers. Rather, these secondary markets stimulate interest and leave many people wanting the total experience of those movies. And, in turn, this desire to see films on "the big screen" will lead them to the archives for a night in the theater.

There they will discover that archives are not dead storage. Whether projected at the Museum of Modern Art in New York City or in Melnitz Hall on UCLA's campus, these preserved films come alive again on the big screen. With more and more preserved and restored films to show, Rosen sees a lively and expanding role for the archives.

Restored by the UCLA Film and Television Archive, *My Man Godfrey* (1936) was directed by Gregory La Cava. The film is a funny, fanciful look at the Great Depression and features the screwball comedy talents of William Powell and Carole Lombard.

"These films represent our distinctive artistic product. They are our distinctive document, our distinctive heritage. To convince people abstractly of the need for preservation is difficult. But when you actually experience one of these films, on a big screen, with a beautiful restored print, in a darkened theater, you fall in love with the image and come to feel in your gut the tragedy of what might have been lost."
—Robert Rosen
Photo: Phillip Channing. Courtesy, UCLA Film and Television Archive.

Preservationist Eric Aijala, a specialist in restoring silent-era films, shelves a reel in a storage vault at the UCLA Film and Television Archive. *The Sea Hawk* (1924), which was showcased during UCLA's 1994 Preservation Festival, was one of his projects. The 1995 Preservation Festival featured new 35mm prints of other films restored by Aijala and his colleague Rosa Castro—*A Man for All Seasons* (Fred Zinnemann's award-winning film); the Frank Capra comedy *Meet John Doe;* and two Sherlock Holmes titles starring Basil Rathbone and Nigel Bruce. Funding was provided by Hugh Hefner. *Photo: Blaine M. Bartell. Courtesy, Eric Aijala.*

As repertory houses decline, as studios are disinclined to make prints and prefer to release films in video versions, the archive will be virtually the last place that you can see the original film. . . .

Fifty years from now, when the only way to see an original print will be in an archival setting, the print will still be looking good. Archives will truly become the equivalent of museums for painting.

The National Archives   In September 1926 when $6.9 million was allocated for a National Archives building, Will H. Hays, former postmaster general and president of the Motion Picture Producers and Distributors of America, proposed that the new building should contain twenty film vaults, each one with a capacity for one thousand reels of film.

On June 19, 1934, an act of Congress created the National Archives and Records Administration for newsreels and government films.

Today a new National Archives building built to the highest current standards—"Archives II"—has been opened in College Park, Maryland. It stores color film at 25°F and at 30 percent relative humidity. The vaults also contain an air filtration system to cut down on pollutants.

Following nitrate fires in the late 1970s in its Maryland storage vaults, the archive received increased support to copy the federal nitrate holdings. By the mid-1980s all of the National Archives' nitrate was copied onto 16mm safety film. Today the archive encourages federal agencies to place government-made films under archival conditions soon after production.

According to Lewis Bellardo, director of the archives' Preservation Policy and Services Division, the National Archives is currently duplicating materials at a rate of about two million feet per year, trying to stay ahead of "the curve of deterioration."

Although the National Archives is primarily responsible for holding "the official records of all media of the federal government," it is also responsible for the safekeeping of documentary materials, including two titles listed on the National Film Registry: *The River* (1937) and *The Battle of San Pietro* (1945).

Using Army Signal Corps footage of the fierce fighting between German and American troops for a minor military objective in Italy during World War II, John Huston wrote and narrated a moment-to-moment account of the combat. *The Battle of San Pietro* (1945) shows the horror of war and its effect on soldiers and civilians alike.
Photo: The Museum of Modern Art/Film Stills Archive.

Other American Archives . . .

These major institutions are by no means the only archives in the United States. Many regional museums, universities, and archives store motion picture footage—millions of feet of it. Among these are the Academy Film Archive, which the Academy Foundation of the Academy of Motion Picture Arts and Sciences has operated since the 1970s. The purpose of its collection, according to the archive's director Michael Friend, is to "serve the work of the Academy and foster the study of the motion picture."

The Academy's archive has over twelve thousand films and videotapes, many of which are Academy Award winners and nominees, as well as filmed records of the Academy Awards ceremonies. It also contains gifts of personal collections from prominent Hollywood figures such as directors Alfred Hitchcock, Fred Zinnemann, John Huston, and Sam Peckinpah.

One of the country's most important medium-sized archives is the Pacific Film Archive of the University Art Museum at the University of California, Berkeley. Specializing in independent and avant-garde films, the archive holds a significant collection of Japanese and Soviet films. The latter are now categorized as Russian, Ukrainian, and Georgian cinema. It also collects historical film of the San Francisco Bay Area.

According to General Manager Stephen Gong, the Pacific Film Archive presents "one of the most extensive exhibition programs in the country with over 650 film and video screenings annually to a total audience of more than 55,000."

These programs range from silent films accompanied by live music to premieres

Once a newsreel had played the theaters, it was disassembled and individual stories were used as stock footage. As a result, most newsreel projects require extensive restoration.
UCLA has housed the Hearst Metrotone News Collection since 1982. Its eleven million feet of nitrate film include coverage of the 1939 Atlanta premiere of *Gone With the Wind* on December 14, 1939. Clark Gable, who played Rhett Butler, and his wife, actress Carole Lombard, are seen here among the prominent attendees.
Photo: UCLA's Hearst Metrotone News Collection.

of experimental film and video art. Designed as a film library and study center, the archive's sixty-five thousand titles are mostly viewing prints, both 16mm and 35mm, rather than archival-quality preservation masters.

Other regional archives include: The Wisconsin Center for Film and Theater Research, which makes viewing prints of pre-1950 Warner Bros., RKO, and Monogram films available to students and scholars; the Northeast Historic Film Society in northern New England, which houses over 1.5 million feet of regional film; and the Southwest Film/Video Archives in Dallas, Texas, which specializes in independent and African-American films.

The fledgling Association of Moving Image Archivists (AMIA) serves as a network among these smaller and regional archives. Much as FIAF, the International Federation of Film Archives, has served as the link between major international archives since 1938, AMIA's objective is to exchange information and ideas about preservation among archives. It also strives to promote archival activities, to encourage public awareness, and to establish professional standards and practices for the preservation of the moving image.

This nonprofit corporation meets yearly and publishes a bimonthly newsletter to exchange information and expertise about preservation. The American Film Institute's National Center for Film and Video Preservation serves as secretariat for the association.

The American Film Institute and The National Center for Film and Video Preservation

I think we have a tremendous responsibility as a nation to save these images. —*Jean Picker Firstenberg, director, American Film Institute*

During the 1993 Library of Congress hearings on film preservation, George Stevens, Jr., remembered how he first became aware of the crisis American film was facing at the 1963 Cannes Film Festival.

Henri Langlois [founder of the Cinémathèque Française] accosted me, sat down and started this tirade about the failure of America to preserve its films. I was very ignorant of those circumstances and he was a missionary preserving films in Europe, but he also had this great love and affection for American films and it was provocative and stimulating.

In the immediately ensuing years when we were planning the American Film Institute, it certainly put preservation at the forefront of my mind and made it a cornerstone when the AFI was founded.

In the early 1960s, according to Stevens, the studios had "virtually no interest" in film preservation. Stevens and actor Gregory Peck, the founding chairman of the AFI, made several trips to Washington, D.C., to testify before Congress, presenting the preservation problem.

On September 26, 1965, President Lyndon B. Johnson announced: "We will create an American Film Institute, bringing together leading artists of the film industry, outstanding educators, and young men and women who wish to pursue the twentieth century's art form as their life's work."

President Johnson's enthusiasm for the undertaking helped gain a grant from the NEA, which, in tandem with Ford Foundation money and more than a million dollars from the Motion Picture Association of America, provided initial funding for the AFI. The private, nonprofit corporation's establishment was announced in June 1967.

The decision was made not to create another archive. George Eastman House, the Library of Congress, the Museum of Modern Art, and the National Archives were already active and growing. Instead, the AFI was designed as a "clearinghouse"—a sort of centralized institution to coordinate and stimulate regional activities. George Stevens, Jr., was named the institute's director and chief executive officer. The new institute quickly discovered that one of the most pressing problems for the film industry and for the public archives was preservation.

"Our national film heritage was in imminent danger of disintegration," says Jean Picker Firstenberg, who has been director of the American Film Institute since 1980.

Between 1968 and 1971 the AFI deposited nearly eight thousand films at the Library of Congress, and by 1993 the AFI had delivered over twenty-five thousand films, which are held at the Library of Congress and other archives.

Because the bulk of the American Film Institute Collection was to be housed at the Library of Congress, the first priority became to fill the gap in the Library's collection—

American Film Institute

AFI's logo reminds the public that both the past and the future of the art of motion pictures must be fostered.
Photo: Courtesy, The American Film Institute.

**Advancing and preserving
the art of the moving image**

films released between 1912 and 1942. The first major AFI acquisition to go to the Library
of Congress in January 1969 was the entire RKO feature library.

In December 1967 the AFI published a "rescue list," naming 250 American films
that were believed to be lost or in serious danger of decay. These included well-known
titles such as *Stagecoach* (1939) and *The Front Page* (1931) and lesser-known titles like
The Girl from Montmartre (1926) and *Washington Merry-Go-Round* (1932).

Over the years there has been criticism of the institute. Its detractors claim that
AFI's focus on publicity overshadows its direct efforts for preservation. The AFI maintains a high profile with the general public through its publications; its Los Angeles–based
campus, the Center for Advanced Film Studies; its annually televised "Life Achievement
Award" show; its film theater at the Kennedy Center in Washington, D.C.; and its successful promotion of restored classics like Abel Gance's *Napoleon* (1927) and *Lawrence
of Arabia* (1962).

However, the AFI does raise funds specifically for preservation. On October 23,
1974, the institute organized National Film Day. Over four thousand movie theaters donated
half their box-office receipts for that day to the AFI for film preservation. In June 1983
the institute launched "The Decade of Preservation," a ten-year-long campaign to raise
both awareness and funds.

In January of 1984 the National Center for Film and Video Preservation began
operation as a separate AFI entity, funded by the AFI and the National Endowment for
the Arts. Its purpose was to assume and continue the work begun by the AFI in 1967
in the area of film acquisition and grants administration. The center operates autonomously
in offices on the AFI's Los Angeles campus and in Washington, D.C.

Today it is the center's primary job to promote the collection and preservation of
film. It is actively involved in the ongoing acquisition of film, adding to the growing body
of titles in the Library of Congress. In recent years one of the largest finds consisted of
over five hundred cans of nitrate film that had been stored in a Michigan barn for over

Bronco Billy Anderson was America's first cowboy star. When two of his films produced by Essanay were found among the Australian gift, film historians were thrilled. Only 10 percent of Essanay's product has survived the twentieth century, making even two titles a very significant find.
Photo: The Museum of Modern Art/Film Stills Archive.

The Australian Gold Mine

In August of 1994, Australia's National Film and Sound Archive gave some very important film history back to the United States. Five tons of film—over 1,500 nitrate-stock titles, many of them thought to be lost forever—were donated to AFI's National Center for Film and Video Preservation in Washington, D.C.

The fact that these films, dating from the early 1900s through the 1950s, had survived "Down Under" did not completely surprise American archivists. Australia was traditionally the "last stop" in the U.S. distribution chain for entertainment films.

Ann Baylis, acting director for the Australian archive, said, "We are sorry to part with these films but we would not have been able to preserve them for at least twenty years. By that time they could have decomposed. This was the only responsible course for us to take. We believe very strongly in working together within the international archiving community."

This required not only international cooperation, but also cooperation among the American archives. "No one archive working alone could have possibly undertaken this repatriation—and, only by working together, can the American archives hope to save this invaluable legacy," commented UCLA Archive curator Eddie Richmond.

The titles were distributed to the major American archives, including George Eastman House, the Library of Congress, and the Museum of Modern Art, and while the cost to store and preserve this gold mine is daunting, these institutions and others accepted the challenge. They even paid their share of the shipping costs.

Among the golden nuggets were trailer footage from an otherwise lost film directed by Ernst Lubitsch, *The Patriot* (1925), and a previously lost Harold Lloyd short, *Peculiar Patients' Pranks* (1915).

Initially AFI National Center archivist Susan Dalton believed the collection contained two Lloyd shorts. It turned out that

Once Every Ten Minutes, also released in 1915, which has long been credited as a Lloyd picture, was not. Only a find like this could reveal the truth and set the record straight, proving that film history *must* be written using primary source material (the films themselves) rather than relying on secondary sources.

While most of the films are "orphans," the collection also contains a treasure trove of Twentieth Century–Fox negative and printing elements, including such popular titles as *The Call of the Wild* and *How Green Was My Valley.*

Dalton called the repatriation a "wealth of treasures," and at least for Harold Lloyd's granddaughter, Susan Lloyd Hayes, it was a personal joy as well as a collective one. "To regain some of my grandfather's work after nearly eighty years is miraculous," she said when the find was announced. "All Americans who love film will benefit from this gift."

fifty years. Saved in April 1987, these films are now the Uhl Collection held at the Library of Congress.

Robert Uhl, a student at the University of Toledo, was aware that his grandfather had film stored in a barn and informed his film history professor. Together with a group of students, they drove to Michigan and hauled the film down to Toledo. They temporarily stored the cans in an old building on the campus, where they soon discovered that many cans were filled with disintegrated nitrate stock. Aware of the danger this posed, they decided to call for help.

Paul Spehr, usually based in Washington, D.C., happened to be at the Library of Congress's Conservation Center in Dayton when a call came in from the University of Toledo. With colleague George Willeman, Spehr drove to Toledo to inspect the film.

The first thing Spehr and Willeman did was get the cans out of the basement of the wooden building where they were being stored. "The place was a tinderbox," recalls Spehr. "And there was enough deterioration that the film needed to get into vaults—immediately." Since the Library of Congress is the repository for the AFI's films, and because the AFI's National Center for Film and Video Preservation is an independent agency comparatively free of bureaucracy and can operate quickly, Susan Dalton, director of Preservation and Archival Projects, was called to retrieve the film.

In the style of a silent film melodrama, Dalton conducted an emergency rescue operation in virtually one day. She flew from Washington, D.C., to Ohio, rented a truck, loaded the cans, and drove down I-75 to the Conservation Center in Dayton with her cargo of deteriorating nitrate.

During World War I or the early 1920s, someone in the Uhl family had worked in film distribution. The collection was well organized and labeled and on proper reels. The bulk of the footage were titles from the 1910s and 1920s and was non-Hollywood product or films produced by companies no longer in business by the 1920s—the type of material that an independent film distributor would have, says Spehr.

Although close to half of the material had to be discarded because of deterioration, the salvageable footage contained part of *The Italian* (1915), produced by pioneer Thomas Ince. Paul Spehr remembers:

> Of a five-reel film, there was less than two-and-one-half reels that could be saved. In the Library's collection, we had the complete paper print version and two reels of actual film. As coincidence would have it, the two reels we already had in the collection were the first two and the two we got in the Uhl Collection, I think, were the third and the fourth.

An important Ince production, *The Italian* is particularly interesting because it was shot on location in the streets of New York and on the canals of Venice, California, capturing and documenting two fascinating sites of the time. In 1991 the film was added to the National Film Registry, and in 1994 the Library finished a stunning restoration.

Beginning in 1967 the AFI/NEA Film Preservation Program annually awarded grants totaling more than $350,000 for the preservation of unique or best-surviving copies of motion pictures.

Archives qualified for support by demonstrating a movie's cultural value and rarity. To receive funds they were required to offer a preservation plan, including laboratory estimates, and match whatever federal money was assigned to the project with local funds on at least a dollar-for-dollar basis. Like many federal arts grants, these applications were reviewed by a panel of experts in the field.

The Italian (1915) was one of many films preserved by the Library of Congress in 1994 at their laboratory in Dayton, Ohio. Despite the serendipity of the print found in the Michigan barn, the film's restoration was based almost entirely on a surviving paper print, which was in superb condition. The nitrate footage did supply the material for a very short scene that was partially missing in the paper records.

The Italian was produced by Thomas Ince, and its star George Beban was praised for his underplayed performance. Filmed on location in New York and California, the photography was impressive for its day, and the movie is interesting not only as an advancement of the art of the motion picture but also for its documentary qualities.

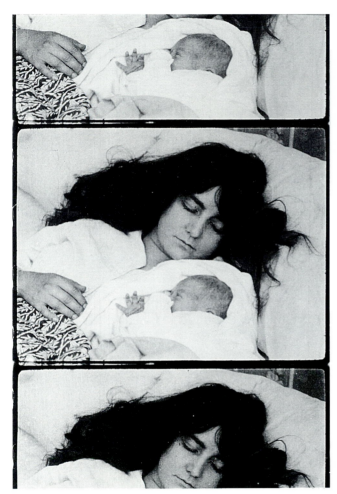

Clara Williams as Annette.
Photo: Ken Weissman.

George Beban (Beppo) dances in the street when he learns of the birth of his child.
Photo: Ken Weissman.

Between 1979 and 1992, half of the film titles saved by money distributed through the AFI/NEA grants were silent nitrate films made before 1929. In recent years, the AFI/NEA monies have begun to fund the copying of decaying acetate film as well. The program was halted in 1995 when the NEA's budget was cut by $2.9 million and chairwoman Jane Alexander terminated all of its subgrant programs. These included the AFI/NEA Film Preservation Grant Program as well as the AFI's Independent Film and Videomakers Grant Program. The AFI director Jean Firstenberg commented on the loss of funds:

> For twenty-seven years the American Film Institute has been proud to administer both these programs. The flow-through grants have been a lifeline for the archives in America and for independent artists. The consequences of these

policy changes are particularly intense for this young American art form that clearly does not have the same history of philanthropic support given to the traditional art forms. . . .

This change in NEA policy will force monumental changes in archival policies in the fight to preserve our country's moving image heritage. The "orphan" movie, a film without a copyright owner, has neither a structure nor a home to ensure its preservation. Our moving image heritage—American's contribution to the world of art—deserves this nation's respect and financial commitment.

Indeed, the preservation program has had an impressive history, granting more than $9.5 million to a variety of specialized film collections and state and regional archives, as well as to the major national archives.

Although the AFI/NEA Film Preservation Program, as it existed, was terminated in 1994, the outcry from the film preservation community resulted in productive discussions with NEA. As a result direct grants were created. UCLA, for example, received a $50,000 direct grant from NEA in 1995. The archive announced that it would use the funds to support the preservation of rare motion pictures in three categories: silent features produced between 1917 and 1929, two Harold Lloyd comedies, and animated cartoons by Ub Iwerks and George Pal. In 1995 UCLA was also awarded a $95,000 AFI Challenge Grant for Film Preservation.

The National Center for Film and Video Preservation also supervises the publication of the *AFI Catalog of Feature Films.* When completed the *Catalog* will provide definitive filmographies on a decade-by-decade basis for all feature-length motion pictures produced in the United States, whether or not they survive. The catalog project, funded by the NEA, the David and Lucile Packard Foundation, and other individuals and foundations, began in 1969. Volumes covering the 1910s, 1920s, 1930s, and 1960s are completed, and *Film Beginnings, 1893–1910* was published in April 1995. The 1940s volume is in process, and preliminary research has been completed on the 1950s.

The *Catalog* provides preservationists with a unique, supplementary source for the historical documentation of films. These definitive entries are based on studio production records, corporate documents, state and local censorship film documents, and the films themselves.

The 1930s volume, for example, provides new and more accurate information on the exact number of films surviving from that decade. The catalog documents that features from the 1930s may have a survival rate of close to 90 percent compared to the fewer than 20 percent that survive from the 1920s. The *AFI Catalog* staff viewed 79 percent of the 5,250 feature films produced in America between 1931 and 1940 and confirmed the existence of more.

Also located on the AFI's Los Angeles campus is the National Moving Image Database (NAMID)—a central computer system that collects and processes information about the archival holdings of institutions and producers. As of April 1993, NAMID had over 165,000 records in its database, gathered from twenty-one participating institutions. These entries covered approximately one hundred thousand feature films, short subjects, videos, and avant-garde films.

Access to the database, however, is limited and complex. Only a fraction of it is available for direct, dial-in consultation, and delays in updating information have made archivists reluctant to use NAMID. Currently, archivists still prefer to contact each other directly to exchange information.

The Center for Advanced Film and Television Studies is located on AFI's Los Angeles campus. There, as many as two hundred fellows (of all ages) are trained annually in film and video techniques. The campus is also home to NAMID, the National Moving Image Database, and the offices of the *AFI Catalog*. *Photo: Courtesy, The American Film Institute.*

American Film Institute 1967–1992: Highlights from the First Twenty-five Years

1967: Work begins to locate and preserve a list of 250 rare and historically important American films.

1969: Center for Advanced Film and Televison Studies opens its Los Angeles campus.

1973: Director John Ford receives the first annual Life Achievement Award.

1973: The AFI Theatre opens at the John F. Kennedy Center in Washington, D.C.

1974: The Directing Workshop for Women is initiated with funding from the Rockefeller Foundation.

1975: AFI launches its magazine, *American Film.*

1976: The second volume of *The American Film Institute Catalog: Feature Films 1961–1970* is published.

1979: "The Best Remaining Seats"— a program that runs classic films in historic movie palaces—is launched in Los Angeles.

1981: The new AFI campus in Los Angeles opens, thanks to a $1 million gift from the Louis B. Mayer Foundation and a $500,000 donation from trustee Mark Goodson.

1984: The National Center for Film and Video Preservation is created.

1987: The first annual AFI International Film Festival is held in Los Angeles, with over one hundred filmmakers from more than twenty nations in attendance.

1989: Successful premieres of the restored version of *Lawrence of Arabia* raise funds for the AFI.

Among NAMID's records are over twenty-two thousand extensively detailed files from the Library of Congress's nitrate film inventory system and eight thousand inventory-level records from the Pacific Film Archives at the University of California, Berkeley.

Iris Barry's interest, intelligence, and enthusiasm for "film as art" provided a springboard for the appreciation and preservation of motion pictures in the United States. For many film lovers, Barry is a symbol of the passion to keep the history of film vital and alive for future generations. Today archivists and film preservationists continue to be inspired by the work she began in the 1930s and a gratified public goes on reaping the rewards.

CHAPTER 5

The Hollywood Studios and Preservation

> How could movies be taken seriously if they were to remain so ephemeral, so lacking in pride of ancestry or of tradition?
> —*Iris Barry, first curator, Museum of Modern Art Film Library*

In August of 1935 Iris Barry went to Hollywood in search of support from the motion picture industry for the Museum of Modern Art's new Film Library. Accompanied by John Hay Whitney, one of MoMA's trustees and an independent film producer, Barry made her appeal to a small gathering of motion picture producers at Pickfair, the lavish home built by silent stars Mary Pickford and Douglas Fairbanks. Her goal was to convince the Hollywood elite to deposit their "product" in a museum.

At that time, the industry viewed copies of old movies primarily as a liability. From the studios' point of view, films were disposable products. But unlike other disposable products, beaten-up and worn-out release prints came back to the studio. Keeping these "useless" prints on the shelf was costly; used nitrate's value lay in melting it down for its silver content.

Only a few producers and studios regularly re-released titles. There was little or no market for an average movie after it had played in the theaters, and technology was consistently making old films obsolete. When sound came in, silent pictures were passé. In 1932 the introduction of three-strip Technicolor threatened the use of black and white.

On top of all this, it was dangerous to store nitrate. Logically, many studios simply destroyed their old product.

It was Iris Barry's intention to communicate the artistic and cultural value of motion pictures to a group who thought much more like manufacturers than like artists. That summer night in 1935, she succeeded in changing a few minds with her presentation of film clips from important American movies. They included *The Great Train Robbery* (1903), as well as scenes from D. W. Griffith's *The New York Hat* (1912), starring hostess Mary Pickford, and Charlie Chaplin's *The Gold Rush* (1925).

This was the beginning of MoMA's close relationship with Hollywood, and the Film Library received its first donations: eleven films from Harold Lloyd, eleven from Warner

Iris Barry (far right) in 1935 in the company of some of Hollywood's elite. From left to right: Frances Howard (Mrs. Samuel Goldwyn), John "Dick" Abbott (Barry's husband), Samuel Goldwyn, Mary Pickford, Jesse Lasky, and Harold Lloyd.
Photo: The Museum of Modern Art/Film Stills Archive.

Bros., seven from Twentieth Century–Fox, two from Samuel Goldwyn, and some early shorts from Walt Disney. Barry also secured verbal promises from Columbia, RKO, Universal, and Mary Pickford, among others.

Barry recalled in 1941:

> That evening, pioneers of the industry like Mack Sennett met newcomers like Walt Disney for the first time, old acquaintances were renewed and new ones made. . . . This glimpse of the birth and growth of an art which was peculiarly their own both surprised and moved this unique audience. . . . At the close of the program, Will H. Hays and Mary Pickford endorsed the Film Library's undertaking in enthusiastic speeches. Samuel Goldwyn and Harold Lloyd as well as Miss Pickford promised their films.

The Great Train Robbery (1903) was one of the films Iris Barry showed to a special group at Pickfair in 1935 to convince them that film was "art."
Photo: The Museum of Modern Art/Film Stills Archive.

By 1936 an astonishing agreement had been reached with Paramount Pictures and M-G-M that allowed the Film Library to make prints that could be used for educational purposes. This meant that, for the first time, movies could be viewed outside the commercial arena. Most of the other major studios also signed the agreement, and "film studies" in the United States was launched with MoMA's circulating library.

Despite Barry's inroads, it took many more years for most of Hollywood's producers to see the value in preserving motion pictures. With the advent of television and video, those markets demanded product and were initially satisfied with less-than-perfect copies.

Columbia Pictures, for example, hastily transferred its best titles, such as *It Happened One Night* (1934), to safety material and then destroyed the nitrate. The studio did not want to spend the money to copy their less popular titles. So these were simply left on the original nitrate. As a result, today, in many cases, Columbia has inferior acetate duplications of its classic films, and quality original material to use to preserve its run-of-the-mill films.

It was only in the 1980s that the majority of the studios had to meet new and much higher standards when it came to making copies of older movies. Foreign television, cable, and home video markets demanded high-quality, original materials from which to make video masters.

The introduction of high-resolution television revealed the vast inadequacies of the "dupey," muddy, poor-definition 16mm prints that had shown for decades on late-night TV. And cable has demonstrated beyond a doubt that there is a substantial audience for uncut and uninterrupted Hollywood classics.

Lew Ayres and Louis Wolheim in *All Quiet on the Western Front* (1930). When Barry showed some of the film at Pickfair: "There was a tiny, shocked gasp at the first appearance of Louis Wolheim. . . . He had been dead so very short a time. Was fame so brief? Of course there ought to be a museum of the film!" In 1996 the Library of Congress completed a restoration of the film. *Photo: The Museum of Modern Art/Film Stills Archive. Courtesy, MCA Publishing Rights, a Division of MCA Inc. Copyright © Universal City Studios, Inc.*

American Movie Classics (AMC), a cable channel that began operation in 1984, has been a particular friend to preservation. One of AMC's strengths is that it not only airs unaltered classic feature films, but also re-creates the *total* movie-going experience of the 1930s and 1940s with newsreels, short subjects, previews of coming attractions, and cartoons, delivered to the viewer's living room.

In March 1993 AMC launched its first Film Preservation Festival in conjunction with The Film Foundation. As part of its fund-raising drive, the station aired classic feature films that had been restored to mint condition. These included the national television premiere of the Technicolor milestone *Becky Sharp* (1935), Chaplin's silent masterpiece *The Gold Rush* (1925), the suspense classic *Laura* (1944), and Marlene Dietrich

As of 1996, American Movie Classics has raised over $1 million for film preservation collected from dedicated AMC viewers. CEO Josh Sapan feels that keeping our movie heritage alive is vital to our national sense of self. "Art defines a culture," says Sapan. "And the power of a people's art and culture can serve to keep its spirit alive in the face of prejudice and discrimination."
Photo: Courtesy, American Movie Classics.

as *The Scarlet Empress* (1934). AMC also aired UCLA-restored Betty Boop cartoons and the Library of Congress–preserved Bugs Bunny cartoons, as well as newsreels from UCLA's Hearst Metrotone News Collection.

For the event, AMC produced mini-documentaries illustrating the efforts of America's foremost film archives, as well as the topical documentaries *Nitrate Won't Wait* and *The Wizards of Preservation.*

AMC received more than fifty-five hundred calls and raised over $300,000 during the festival. Approximately $220,000 of this was distributed to the five archives by The Film Foundation, which acted as a clearinghouse for the funds as well as a consultant for the festival. UCLA's Film and Television Archive, for example, received $44,000 as its share of the net proceeds, a sum dedicated to the preservation and restoration of specific films.

During the 1960s and 1970s, art houses and revival theaters across the country provided important showcases for preserved films. In Los Angeles the Vagabond, a revival house, frequently showed prints from UCLA's archive. When the video and cable market exploded in the 1980s, many of these theaters were put out of business, including the Vagabond, owned by Tom Cooper. His final bill in November 1985 was "The Best of Warner Bros. Cartoons."

During Cooper's ten years, the Vagabond hosted many famous guests, from 1940s siren Rita Hayworth to director George Cukor. A popular guest was M-G-M musical director Charles Walters. The theater attracted celebrities as patrons as well, including directors François Truffaut and Steven Spielberg. Gene Kelly would frequently sneak in for his favorite Buster Keaton films.

According to film historian Ron Haver, revival theaters died off because of competition from home video and because exhibitors were increasingly reluctant to pay high rental and transportation prices for "spliced, scratched, and faded prints." The studios, on the other hand, felt it made no sense to spend thousands of dollars making a new print that might never return its cost in rental fees.

Despite the decline in the number of screens, according to Paramount's Michael Schlesinger, as of 1990 there were fifty to sixty "prime" repertory houses in operation nationwide. He also stated that they were "starved" for pristine-quality prints.
Photo: Joanne Yeck.

Following the success of the first festival, AMC announced plans to make it an annual event. The second festival, in October 1994, focused on Westerns and aired some of the titles restored with funds raised in 1993. The summer 1996 festival featured musicals.

A very significant supporter of American film preservation is the David and Lucile Packard Foundation. Between 1981 and 1992, the Packard Foundation distributed over $2 million for film copying, exhibition, and research to the National Center for Film and Video Preservation, the Library of Congress, the Pacific Film Archive, and the UCLA Film and Television Archive.

According to UCLA lecturer and film collector Bob Epstein, foundation trustee David Packard got excited about film preservation when he saw some archival prints shown at the Vagabond Theatre in Los Angeles. "Packard was amazed at how good these movies looked," says Epstein. "He became a major benefactor of the archive."

The David and Lucile Packard Foundation gave major support for the preservation of Frank Capra films at the Library of Congress, and its recent gift of a new printer for the Library's Dayton center has made that facility "world-class."

The Packard Foundation has also been a major funder of the *AFI Catalog* and the conversion of nitrate newsreels and classic feature films at UCLA. These include a wide range of titles, from *Life with Father* (1947), the Technicolor feature based on the popular play by Howard Lindsay and Russel Crouse, to *Follow Thru* (1930), a two-color Technicolor musical starring Buddy Rogers and Nancy Carroll, and the 1929 version of *The Virginian,* starring a very young Gary Cooper.

The Packard Foundation is particularly concerned with the public's access to film as the vital end result of preservation, and has supported the striking of new 35mm prints so the public can experience films as they were intended to be seen.

According to Robert Rosen, preservation need no longer be a purely philan-thropic endeavor: "People around the world have discovered that their holdings are not dead storage but are in fact capital assets. So preservation is no longer an esoteric process. We're at a turning point in which the industry is realizing the economic value of putting those beautiful films back up on the screen."

The restoration of *Lawrence of Arabia* cost $600,000, and its profits for Columbia Pictures exceeded $2 million. The restoration of *Gone With the Wind* cost $350,000, and it generated a $7 million profit for Turner Entertainment. When the restored *The Wiz-ard of Oz* sold three million videocassettes, it netted $10 million.

With profits like these, the preservation of such films *isn't* a philanthropic endeavor. Yet there are only a handful of titles that can bring in this kind of money. Motion pic-ture studios are in business and need some economic motivation to preserve film. Not every preserved film has to sell a million videocassettes, but there must be a reasonable return to the company to encourage preservation.

Turner Entertainment president and CEO Roger Mayer feels that the studios need to preserve their libraries fully prior to the lapse of copyright. "There are films falling out of protection," says Mayer. "And if we could get an extension of this protection, the economic advantages of spending the money certainly would be much more forthright." He also points out that while copyright protection may have lapsed in the United States, a company could still have protection in foreign markets. This can be a motive to continue preservation efforts.

Today, Hollywood studios and production companies—the copyright holders of thousands of titles of classic American movies—are fully aware of their market potential. "There's gold in those old film cans," says Mayer.

Turner Entertainment currently owns a large share of this pot of gold, includ-ing a rich collection of M-G-M, Warner Bros., and RKO classics. The company suc-cessfully capitalizes on these films on cable via its satellite stations TBS, TNT, and Turner Classic Movies (TCM), which follows the design of its predecessor, AMC, airing clas-sics, Turner-produced documentaries about Hollywood, and shorts. They all run uninterrupted. TCM's great advantage is the fabulous Turner-owned library, a welcome boon for old-movie lovers. On videocassette, Turner offers both restored classics and such items as deluxe anniversary editions of favorites like *Gone With the Wind* and *Casablanca.*

As Mary Lea Bandy, chief curator of the Museum of Modern Art Film Library exults, "So, the wheel comes full circle for the film companies, and literally everything they have is turning out to be of interest. Thank God, they put the stuff in the archives!"

Roger L. Mayer, president and chief operating officer, Turner Entertainment Co.
Photo: Courtesy, Roger Mayer.

Roger Mayer: Ambassador for Film Preservation

In 1995 Roger Mayer, president and chief operating officer of Turner Entertainment Co., was awarded the International Documentary Association's Preservation and Scholarship Award. Joining illustrious past recipients, including UCLA's Robert Rosen, silent film expert David Shepard, and paper print preservationist Kemp Niver, Mayer was dubbed "a tireless spokesman and goodwill ambassador for the important cause of preservation."

After twenty-five years at M-G-M, Mayer moved to Turner Entertainment, where he is responsible for Hollywood's most impressive film library. His commitment to preservation goes beyond his own library; he serves as a member of the National Film Preservation Board as well as the Academy Foundation of the Academy of Motion Picture Arts and Sciences.

"Preservation is taken seriously now in Hollywood," says Mayer. "The only real assets of a motion picture company are its films. But they only retain value (historical, artistic, and commercial) if they're stored properly and handled wisely."

In addition to Turner's $1.5 million per year commitment to maintain its library, the company has projected an estimated seven-year project to re-preserve 120 films that were originally shot in three-strip Technicolor. Advances in technology since these films were first transferred to safety stock now warrant making new preservation masters.

As far as Turner Entertainment is concerned, Mayer concludes, "There is no distinction between a good or bad, successful or unsuccessful film. We simply do them all."

The beautiful results of Turner preservation and restoration can be seen around the clock without commercial interruption on Turner Classic Movies cable station. The recent restorations of M-G-M classic color musicals *The Harvey Girls* and *Seven Brides for Seven Brothers,* for example, are welcome treasures for TCM viewers.

In the past the motion picture industry may have been slow to recognize the importance of maintaining its product, but today many studios are full partners with public archives in preservation efforts. Although studios own the rights to marketable films, they are finding out that, in many cases, they may no longer possess the best elements of the films themselves. The result is that new partnerships are being formed between public institutions and studios, creating a new era of cooperative preservation efforts.

As the guardians of the majority of the post-1950 footage, the studios are taking a new attitude toward their property. Phil Murphy, vice president of operations for the Television Group at Paramount Pictures, points out: "While independent and public archival institutions are also important to maintaining the history of motion pictures, we cannot subrogate our responsibilities to their needs or activities. This is not to say there isn't room for cooperation. We loan material, we finance, we share technological data."

Preservation efforts at major studios share many similarities with those of the public archives. Since the 1980s, most studios have invested millions of dollars in preserving and restoring their copyrighted films.

Many of these millions have been spent on new storage facilities. Like the public archives, studios have accepted that storage at lower temperatures and lower relative humidity makes good economic sense.

Paramount Pictures, one of the leaders in preservation, opened a new $11 million archive building in 1990. The building has cold/dry vaults to house preprint and color materials. Paramount's electric bill alone for its new vault runs to several hundred thousand dollars annually.

In spite of the enormous start-up and maintenance costs for these cold/dry storage units, however, the cost of storing film properly is dramatically cheaper than the cost of continually replicating deteriorating film. By lowering storage temperature from 75°F to 45°F, for instance, color fading that would have occurred in ten years will take closer to one hundred years.

These new archives—the studio-built storage facilities—are state of the art, using UPC code systems to track the location and condition of films. For example, Universal Studios has coded over one million elements, and Paramount tracks its 750,000 items worldwide through an automated inventory system.

Between the end of the 1980s and 1993, Paramount spent over $35 million inspecting its negatives, audio tracks, and color separations. The company spent millions more repairing film and printing new duplicating materials.

Paramount is also actively restoring and exhibiting its classic film library. In time for AFI's 1990 Los Angeles Film Festival, the studio revived *Funny Face* (1957), a color musical starring Fred Astaire and Audrey Hepburn. The film also had a theatrical re-release, and was the fourth-biggest-grossing picture at the AMC Century City 14 Theatres in Los Angeles in its opening week, demonstrating that a *good* movie of any age can draw an audience.

In addition to preserving titles that have commercial value, Paramount is cooperating with the UCLA Film and Television Archive on projects of historical importance, including the transfer of the only theatrical copy of Mary Pickford's *Tess of the Storm Country* (1922) from nitrate to safety stock.

Another major studio, Universal, also works closely with the UCLA Film and Television Archive. The studio and the archive have jointly restored a number of Universal-owned titles, among them *The Phantom of the Opera* (1943) and *The Plainsman* (1936).

For several projects, Universal Pictures/MCA has funded a film's preservation (laboratory costs, stock, etc.) and UCLA has provided the expertise and labor of their archival staff.

Simultaneously, the studio is actively preserving its library, which consists of more than 2,330 theatrical titles and includes Paramount's pre-1948 sound films. Of its 740 color titles, 89 percent are protected with black-and-white separations.

Nitrate conversion is either completed or in process at most of the major studios. M-G-M, which owns approximately fifteen hundred titles including those originally released by United Artists, Cannon, and some smaller companies, is currently remastering its library. Gary Ainsworth, director of film operations at M-G-M, says much of UA's library was in bad shape. As a recent example, Ainsworth cites John Huston's *The Misfits* (1961), starring Clark Gable and Marilyn Monroe. The film is seriously deteriorated, and its surviving elements are currently being evaluated.

Twentieth Century–Fox has converted over eight hundred titles in its library to safety stock. In 1993, Roger Bell, director of administration, Library Services, at Fox, said the studio was "about to embark on a program of redoing the early safety film where the original negative is damaged."

During the decades in which M-G-M owned its very valuable library, the studio was one of the most forward-thinking in terms of preservation. It began converting nitrate titles to safety in the mid-1960s. When Turner Entertainment acquired the M-G-M library in 1986, it inherited this work, plus preservation work done by United Artists while it owned the Warner Bros. pre-1950 library.

Today Turner spends up to $2 million per year maintaining its massive film library, and the company's policy is to protect its titles "one way or another in their entirety without any exceptions," says Roger Mayer. The company's vice president, Richard May, points out the complexity of the task because Turner owns titles that were produced by several studios. Before they were acquired by Turner, the films' original elements had already been donated to a number of institutions, making Turner a potential partner with each of the major archives. According to May:

> All of our original M-G-M negatives are at Eastman House. The Warner and RKO nitrate negatives are at the Library of Congress. The Warner and RKO nitrate fine grains are at the Museum of Modern Art.
>
> I've run into numerous cases where the Library of Congress preserves something, MoMA preserves something, and we already have preservation on the same thing. . . .
>
> Information in order to coordinate and eliminate that duplication and triplication and in sharing those preservation elements, where necessary, between us could add economies that we don't now exercise.

Currently Turner and other studios intentionally separate their preservation materials. They make sure that "preprint" elements—camera negatives, interpositives and duplicating negatives—are stored in at least two diverse geographical locations. California's January 1994 earthquake, which extensively damaged many industry buildings, helped drive home the need for diversified storage.

Studios have "backups" tucked away in a variety of places, from salt mines in Kansas to underground storage in Boyers, Pennsylvania. In Boyers, National Underground Storage safeguards material for Paramount, Columbia, and Disney, and Universal has duplicate negatives of many of its titles there.

Underground Vaults & Storage, Inc., in Hutchinson, Kansas, is the repository for some of America's favorite movies. Its customers include Turner Entertainment, Twentieth Century–Fox, Walt Disney, Columbia Pictures, and United Artists.
Courtesy, Underground Vaults & Storage, Inc.

Sony/Columbia

Studio and Archive Cooperation

We strongly believe a preservation partnership between the major motion pictures studios, film archives, and technical specialists is required.

—*Sony Pictures Entertainment*

In June 1990 senior officers from Sony/Columbia met with representatives of major archives to discuss the preservation of the Columbia Pictures film library. The result was the formation of the Film and Tape Preservation Committee, a model for collaborative efforts between a studio and the public archives.

Under a joint long-term plan Sony/Columbia currently funds preservation work on Columbia titles with the major archives. The studio pays for the cost of lab work, contributes to each archive's staff and research needs, and, if necessary, loans materials to the archive. Following preservation, and in some cases restoration, the archive receives a set of preservation elements and a print to show.

In return Sony/Columbia receives the preserved original materials and from them makes new printing materials. These are used for theatrical re-releases, television, and videocassettes, which ideally earn back the dollars spent on preservation.

Under this program, all partners benefit, significant films are being preserved, and some of the archives' previous financial burden is lifted.

UCLA's partnership with Sony/Columbia actually began in 1988 with the preservation of *Here Comes Mr. Jordan* (1941), the popular fantasy-comedy. More recently, Bob Gitt supervised restoration of *The Guns of Navarone* (1961), which was shot in Eastman Color and had a four-channel stereo sound track.

The Library of Congress has also worked with Sony/Columbia. In 1993 in cooperation with the studio, the Library completed their milestone restoration of Frank Capra's Oscar-winning *Mr. Smith Goes to Washington* (1939). Then in 1996 the Library completed restoration of Capra's Depression-era comedy *Mr. Deeds Goes to Town* (1936). Its next project for Columbia is another film directed by Frank Capra, *The Miracle Woman* (1931), which stars Barbara Stanwyck as an evangelist styled after Aimee Semple McPherson, a flamboyant revivalist of the 1920s.

"It is a model of collaboration for others to follow," says Mary Lea Bandy. "It truly is a collaborative effort by the studios and the archives, who together select the title and mutually agree upon what needs to be done."

Still, the program isn't perfect—yet. "It's a terrific project, although a little slow," adds Bandy. "I think everyone might like to see it speeded up a bit, but considerations of staff, finances, and marketing of the films all have to be taken into account."

Under the Sony/Columbia plan, the Museum of Modern Art's film department has preserved George Stevens's 1943 topical comedy *The More the Merrier* and Elia Kazan's 1954 drama *On the Waterfront* with Marlon Brando, which won eight Oscars, including Best Picture. The cooperative restoration of *On the Waterfront* cost $49,000.

"We chose *On the Waterfront* because it was one of the most important pictures in the Columbia library," says Bandy. "We were also very interested in doing a picture of

The preservation of *On the Waterfront* (1954), starring Marlon Brando and Eva Marie Saint, here with Thomas Handley, was a cooperative project between Sony/Columbia and the Museum of Modern Art. *Photo: The Museum of Modern Art/Film Stills Archive. Copyright © 1954 Columbia Pictures Corporation. All Rights Reserved.*

the early acetate years—a film from the 1950s which was not a nitrate film. I wanted to see what kinds of problems existed with post-nitrate films."

Columbia has made big profits from successful theatrical releases of their restored titles, including *Lawrence of Arabia* (1962), whose earnings far exceeded its preservation costs. This inspired the studio to restore the classic prisoner-of-war film, *The Bridge on the River Kwai* (1957), which had garnered seven Academy Awards, including Best Picture.

Following a limited theatrical run of the restored version, *The Bridge on the River Kwai* was released on videocassette and laser disk in both a "panned-and-scanned" version, which adjusts the CinemaScope image to the television screen, and a "letterbox" version, which preserves the film's original CinemaScope shape.

It took eighteen months and $500,000 to restore the images and the color, and to enhance the film's monaural sound track. Sections of the original color negative had faded, and new footage was derived from the original black-and-white separations.

The results were dramatic. Director David Lean's jungle greens are now revitalized and his rain effects pound down in Dolby stereo. And, most importantly for Columbia's future preservation projects, a new generation of movie lovers is paying the studio back for its efforts.

Eastman House and Turner Entertainment

Like MoMA, Eastman House works closely on joint preservation efforts with several Hollywood studios, including Sony/Columbia, Twentieth Century–Fox, and Turner Entertainment, as well as the French company Gaumont. "The restored versions of *Gone With the Wind* and *The Wizard of Oz,* for example, used our material," explains Chris Horak.

M-G-M donated its Technicolor camera negatives from the 1930s and 1940s to Eastman House in the mid-1970s, making the archive the official repository for many classic color titles, including *Gone With the Wind* and *Meet Me in St. Louis.*

When Turner Entertainment acquired the M-G-M library in the 1980s, the company discovered that many of the Eastman Color duplicate negatives had faded. Now, in cooperation with George Eastman House, Turner is going back to the original Technicolor camera negatives to create new preservation masters.

Eastman House gives Turner access to the archival material, and Turner's preservationists actually do the work. "Sometimes we have the best materials, sometimes Turner has some superior materials—a better sound track, for example," says Horak. "So, we send what we have to a lab in California, they gather all the pieces together and make the print out there."

Warner Bros.: Taking Responsibility

Warner Bros. has decided to handle all of its preservation work "in-house." The studio is protecting all of its new production with black-and-white separations and, says Warner Bros.' vice president Peter Gardiner, "the past will be absolutely taken care of in the same way."

Warner Bros. has built its own state-of-the-art archive on the studio lot. Its technological capabilities set a new industry standard. The archive building has a capacity of approximately six hundred thousand cans of safety film, and the facilities include a gas monitoring device that detects fumes given off when acetate film begins to deteriorate. These vinegar syndrome fumes are tracked by a computer that alerts archivists to the early stages of deterioration. Under such closely guarded conditions,

Margaret O'Brien won a special Oscar for her portrayal of Tootie in the M-G-M Technicolor classic, *Meet Me in St. Louis* (1944). In one of the film's most charming moments, she and Judy Garland sing "Under the Bamboo Tree" for family and friends. The film was named to the National Film Registry in 1994.
Photo: Copyright © 1944 Turner Entertainment Co. All Rights Reserved.

the studio projects a life span of as long as five hundred years for their film library.

With a few exceptions, Warner's film library begins with the Warner titles released after January 1950. The pre-1950 Warner library now belongs to Turner Entertainment. The relatively small amount of nitrate film that Warner Bros. owns was acquired when it bought Lorimar's library, which included Allied Artists' nitrate titles. This footage is stored off the lot, in a separate bunker in Van Nuys, California.

In addition to creating protection copies of all of its titles, Warner Bros. is actively restoring titles for theatrical and video release. The studio's entrance into the preservation field in 1983 was inspired by film historian Ron Haver's passion to restore *A Star Is Born*, the 1954 musical starring Judy Garland and James Mason. The project was supported by the studio and the Academy of Motion Picture Arts and Sciences.

In 1990 Warner Bros. announced the restoration of twenty-six "classics," including *Rebel Without a Cause* (1955), which featured James Dean's quintessential portrayal of alienated youth. Besides preserving important color films such as *East of Eden* (1955), also starring Dean, the studio created an enhanced-sound version of *Woodstock,* the 1970 rock-concert film, which includes extensive footage not seen in the original release.

A Streetcar Named Desire (1951) stars Marlon Brando and Vivien Leigh, who won an Oscar for Best Actress for her performance as Blanche DuBois. The film has been restored to its uncensored length by Warner Bros. and is one of several post–1950 films the studio is releasing on video in the "Warner Bros. Classics" series. Other titles include *Bonnie and Clyde, Dial M for Murder,* and *Rebel Without a Cause.*
Photo: Courtesy, Warner Bros. and Deane Johnson and the Motion Picture and Television Fund.
Copyright © 1951 Charles Feldman Group Productions.

One of the studio's most important restorations to date is a "director's cut" of *A Streetcar Named Desire* (1951). Based on Tennessee Williams's play, this movie's plot involves many highly sensitive elements, including the rape of the heroine. The film challenged Hollywood's strict censorship code and did not escape the censor's scissors. Just before the film's release, about a dozen cuts were made to appease several Catholic organizations that threatened to boycott the picture. The much-feared "C" ("Condemned") rating by the Catholic Legion of Decency was avoided, and the film opened on schedule in the prestigious Radio City Music Hall in New York.

In 1989 Michael Arick, who was then the director of film preservation at Warner Bros., found the cut footage in a mismarked can sitting among some forgotten Westerns. In 1993 Warner Bros. released a stunning "new" *Streetcar* that included the never-before-seen footage. This pristine restored version clearly demonstrates why director Elia Kazan's film was nominated for a dozen Oscars, including one for cinematographer Harry Stradling's beautiful black-and-white camerawork.

Disney Magic: For Generations to Come

The Walt Disney film library is one of the most timeless and beloved collections of motion pictures. The artistic and emotional value of these films have kept them in constant demand generation after generation. The preservation of these films has consequently been of high importance both culturally and corporately, and is a task that has always been approached with serious integrity by the Disney Studio.

—Scott MacQueen, manager, Library Restoration, The Walt Disney Company

Disney's film library is truly a special case in Hollywood's history. Whether it is animated fairy tales like *Cinderella* (1950) and *Sleeping Beauty* (1959) or live-action family classics like *Pollyanna* (1960) and *Mary Poppins* (1964), the timeless nature of so much of Disney's product has kept these titles fresh for generations.

For years, the studio has re-released their animated features on a regular cycle, making these films some of the most profitable of all time. *Bambi* (1942) which cost

Walt Disney greets humorist Robert Benchley, who stars in *The Reluctant Dragon* (1941).
Photo: Copyright © Disney Enterprises, Inc.
With the permission of the Estate of Robert Benchley.

The Reluctant Dragon documents the studio at peak production following the enormous success of *Snow White and the Seven Dwarfs*. This historically important film, unseen in theaters in a complete form since 1941, has been restored by Disney preservationists using three-color Technicolor, Succes-sive Exposure original materials.

In the film, humorist Robert Benchley visits the studio looking for Walt Disney because his wife has insisted he show Kenneth Grahame's charming story "The Reluctant Dragon" to Walt as a possible subject. His search becomes a tour during which Benchley (and the audience) see the marvelous multiplane camera, visit a storyboard session, and get a look at several of the studio's finest animators, including Ward Kimball.

Benchley eventually finds Disney in the projection room ready to screen his newest cartoon featurette—*The Reluctant Dragon*—which then unfolds.

$2 million to make, had generated $100.3 million in domestic releases as of 1990. In 1988 alone, it grossed $39 million. No one would question whether moneymakers like this are worth preserving.

Restoration also focuses on the studio's many cartoon shorts. Restored versions of "Minnie's Yoo-Hoo" (1929) and "The Mail Pilot" (1932) were among those screened at a special Disney tribute at the Twenty-fourth Annual USA Film Festival.

In 1993 Disney gave one of its live-action features, *20,000 Leagues Under the Sea* (1954), a splashy two-week run at Hollywood's historic El Capitan Theater. The film had opened at the El Capitan in December 1954 and won Oscars for its spectacular art direction and for visual effects. Shot in Eastman Color, its negative had begun to fade. The film was restored to its original color; the sound enhanced and remixed for Dolby compatibility.

Disney was among the first Hollywood studios to take a long-term view of its holdings. Its nitrate masters were transferred to safety film in 1962. When Eastman Color was introduced in the early 1950s, the studio wisely made separation masters, thereby protecting its titles against the problems of color-fading.

In 1989 Disney's Buena Vista Visual Effects launched a new preservation program and "re-restored" the entire library to meet contemporary standards. Using wet-gate registered printing, all of the nitrate titles were copied again to safety stock. Disney stores the studio's original nitrate camera negatives with the Library of Congress in Dayton, Ohio.

Breaking New Ground

While many of the studios have flirted with the newest technology for preservation and restoration, Walt Disney Pictures was the first to take the real plunge. Together with Cinesite, an Eastman Kodak company, the studio broke new ground with *Snow White and the Seven Dwarfs* (1937).

In 1937 *Snow White* made history when it became the first feature-length animated film. It premiered on December 21 and was seen by twenty million people within three months, establishing a box-office record in 1938. Before the 1993 re-release, the film had grossed $279 million (not adjusted for inflation).

In 1993 it made history again when it became the first feature-length motion picture to be completely digitalized by computer and then printed back onto film.

Cinesite, located in Hollywood, used a computerized process that scanned the film's 119,550 frames—five trillion pieces of data—and translated them onto digital tape, capturing a single frame every ten seconds. For eighteen weeks more than one hundred artists worked around the clock to refurbish the eighty-two-minute film.

In addition Cinesite cleaned the images with a software program called The Dustbuster, designed to remove dirt and dust from the original negative. This was a lengthy process because the Dustbuster program had to be "told" how to discriminate between animated birds' pupils and dust.

"While it takes only about a minute and a half for the Dustbusting program to 'clean' an individual frame, setting all the parameters can take up to eight hours," explains Bruno George, Cinesite's former creative director. "Defining what constitutes dust and dirt has to be done carefully. If we set the parameters too high, we'd erase all the characters' eyes. So, we had to make sure that the animation was always protected."

Even at that, only about 70 percent of the dirt and grime could be eliminated by the computer. The rest was removed by artists using electronic paint systems that cloned surrounding color. The technicians and artists set out to re-create the experience audiences had in 1937, but they soon discovered that all the defects they were removing were not due to fifty-seven years of decay.

The multiplane animation camera stand was invented for *Snow White*. With it animators were able to give a sense of deep perspective by "stacking" their cels (the individual paintings) in a number of glass layers between the camera lens and the background. This created a realistic, three-dimensional effect. It also trapped dust in the glass platens that held the cels. This debris, affectionately called Disney Dust, was photographed and became part of the image record on the original Technicolor negatives.

Many of these blemishes in the negative went unnoticed in theaters in 1937. Today's audience and projection technology, however, are much sharper and less forgiving when it comes to blemishes. So the Disney/Cinesite goal became to generate a print that would appear flawless by today's standards.

Snow White had been restored by YCM Laboratories for the film's fiftieth anniversary in 1987. At that time, YCM could restore the film's surface, but had no way to change the image. Cinesite's high-resolution digital imaging technology, however, could eliminate the cel dust that had been photographed in 1937. Additionally, it removed most of the film's flicker and flare—flaws also caused by the multiplane stands and embedded in the original Technicolor film.

Once a frame was electronically cleaned and adjusted, it was re-recorded onto film using red, blue, and green laser beams. With the stored digital information, accurate and consistent copies of *Snow White* can be generated with the press of a button.

This digitalization and cleanup wasn't cheap. In fact, at the current prices, few films would be able to make back the cost of this high-tech preservation. A classic Disney animated feature is one of those rare few. The precise cost of *Snow White*'s rejuvenation was never disclosed, but it is estimated to be in the low millions. Re-released on July 2, 1993, *Snow White* had brought in $30 million at the box office by the end of the month.

"Now that *Snow White* exists as a digital code, it is virtually impervious to the ravages of time," says Cinesite president Ed Jones. "When you strike a new negative this

The state-of-the-art Warner Bros. Film Archives facility stores safety-based negative film in vaults that maintain 34–43° F and 28–35 percent humidity. Massive track-mounted film racks make it possible for one person to move more than forty thousand pounds of film by simply turning the wheel located at the end of each rack.
Photo: Copyright © 1995 Warner Bros. Inc. All Rights Reserved.

way, you give a film another one hundred years of life it might not otherwise have—and with the best-quality image current technology can produce."

Best of all, according to Jones, the process fulfills every filmmaker's wish—"that movies can be forever."

Cooperation. Communication. Increased responsibility on the part of copyright holders. The care and protection of "orphan films." These concepts mark an entirely new era in film preservation. **A New Era of Preservation**

With proper storage, a film made today may survive for five hundred years. With an organized agenda for prioritizing preservation, a wide cross section of moving images will be saved for further generations. If properly maintained, these motion pictures will be enjoyed for years to come in archival and revival theaters, as well as in home "theaters"—stored on videotape, laser disk, or new media yet to come.

With more and more individuals, both within and without the motion picture industry, seeing the historic and economic sense behind saving movies, more and more movies *are* being saved.

CHAPTER 6

Other Friends of Preservation

As we move into the twenty-first century,
we may be forced to rethink what preservation means.
—*George Lucas*

Not all film preservation is the result of action by large, bureaucratic institutions. Film-makers, film collectors, and individuals with a vision to save even just one film can make a big difference in the success or failure of film preservation.

Since May 1990 a group of very prominent directors has played a key role in film preservation. The Film Foundation's original board of directors—Martin Scorsese (president), George Lucas, Steven Spielberg, Robert Redford, Sydney Pollack, Woody Allen, Francis Ford Coppola, and Stanley Kubrick—are pledged to increase industry awareness and involvement in the safeguarding of film.

The Film Foundation's members are experienced in making pacts with studios and have offered guidelines for partnerships between public archives and studios. These have been successfully followed by the UCLA Film and Television Archive in establishing cooperative ventures with several studios. Both Sony Pictures Entertainment and Universal Pictures have worked with UCLA using this model.

According to the guidelines, when a title is selected, the archive evaluates both the film elements in its own collection and those provided by the studio, making recommendations which to use for the title's restoration. If the studio agrees and the project goes forward, the studio pays the laboratory costs and both partners retain a set of preprint preservation elements. A number of movies have been restored as a result of these partnerships, including Columbia's *The Wild One* (1954) and Paramount Picture's *Shanghai Express* (1932).

The Film Foundation grew out of director Martin Scorsese's avid personal interest in collection and preservation, which was sparked when his seven-year search for a 35mm print of *The Leopard* (1963) ended in frustration and shock. Scorsese finally located Luchino Visconti's lushly photographed Italian classic in 1979, but the leopard he found was *pink*. The Eastman Color had faded Visconti's vision beyond recognition.

"It's an outrage," Scorsese exclaims. "Making movies has become like writing on

Director/actor Robert Redford, here directing *The Milagro Beanfield War* (1988), is one of the original board members of The Film Foundation. *Photo: Courtesy, MCA Publishing Rights, a Division of MCA Inc. Copyright © 1987 Universal City Studios, Inc.*

water." His outrage led to a one-man investigation of Eastman Color's instability. He discovered that an Eastman Color print can lose its original impact because of color fading in less than eight years, and that a negative, casually stored, can fade in as few as twelve years.

"All of our agonizing labor and creative effort is for nothing, because our films are vanishing," the director said in 1982 as he personally crusaded to save color film.

Scorsese has been one of the most vocal and consistent supporters of film preservation, including the restoration of the epic *El Cid* (1961). In 1991 he was decorated by the French government for his worldwide efforts to save and restore deteriorating films.

"In the end, all we have is our history," agrees Film Foundation co-founder Francis Ford Coppola. "And these films constitute a major portion of the history of the twentieth century."

**Collectors:
Sometimes a Film's Last Hope**

One of the most exciting things for me is to take totally unknown American films, "B" movies or pre-Code films, to places like Austria, Finland, Sweden where they were originally banned, and witness the sense of exhilaration and discovery as critics and audiences discover them for the first time.   —*William K. Everson*

Film enthusiasts and collectors of 16mm film have done much for the cause of preservation. One such individual was historian and collector William K. Everson. "Once in a while when I get into the ocean in Hawaii, or on top of a mountain somewhere, I realize there's something to the world besides film. And for a moment it's overwhelming, but once I get back to earth again, film takes over."

Three generations of friends to preservation: director and preservation activist Martin Scorsese (b. 1942); Eileen Bowser (b. 1928), for many years curator of the Museum of Modern Art's Film Library; and silent screen star Lillian Gish (b. 1896) meet in film historian William K. Everson's living room.
Photo: Courtesy, William K. Everson.

There is no doubt that movies shaped William K. Everson's life. At the age of four, Everson was so impressed with William K. Howard's direction of *Transatlantic* (1931) that he insisted his name be switched from Keith William to William Keith. "But to this day," he admitted in 1985, "my father and my aunts have never accepted me as Bill."

Born in England in 1929, Everson grew up in the town of Hayes, near the site of London's Heathrow Airport. He was only one year old when he saw his first film, probably *The Singing Fool,* the 1928 sequel to *The Jazz Singer* (1927). His mother was an avid moviegoer and took Everson to the cinema every week. Everson vividly remembered the movies he saw after 1932. "The images fascinated me even if I didn't understand them."

Everson began collecting movie magazines even before he could read and saved them until he could. By the time he saw John Ford's *The Whole Town's Talking* (1935) at age six, Everson was fully engaged with the magic of the movies. "Up until that time, I hadn't been paying much attention to dialogue. But because of the film's 'magic,' particularly Edward G. Robinson playing two roles and appearing on screen opposite himself, I was drawn into the plot and really 'discovered' dialogue."

Like some lucky movie enthusiasts, Everson made a career of his passion. Beginning at thirteen, he worked in and around the film business. He authored dozens of books and articles about film history and became the owner of an impressive film collection of more than five thousand features, plus a couple of thousand short subjects.

His collection includes many rare titles, such as *The Second in Command* (1915), starring Francis X. Bushman, a popular matinee idol of the stage and the silent screen. "Rarity does not necessarily indicate quality, of course," admitted Everson. "*The Second in Command* isn't much of a film, but is academically fascinating because of its virtually unprecedented use of the mobile camera. So, it's most useful for teaching, but it's no masterpiece." When Everson acquired a rare title, he always attempted to get it copied by an institution and somehow put back into distribution.

Everson lived in the United States from the late 1950s until his death in 1996. He served as a member of the National Film Preservation Board and taught for many years at New York University's Department of Film and Television. His "road show," "William

Film collector and historian William K. Everson (left) is seen here with Joseph H. Lewis at a retrospective of the director's films in Geneva, Switzerland. Lewis's *Gun Crazy* is a *film noir* cult classic. *Film noir* was a particular favorite of Everson's, along with Westerns, silent sight-gag comedy, and horror films. Everson also specialized in various directors, including James Whale and Maurice Tourneur, whose films *Frankenstein* (1931) and *The Poor Little Rich Girl* (1917) respectively, are on the National Film Registry. *Photo: Courtesy, William K. Everson.*

K. Everson Presents," brought his personal favorites and cinematic rarities to universities and archives such as Berkeley's Pacific Film Archive as well as to London's National Film Theatre, and will long be remembered.

From time to time, Everson was instrumental in saving a title or finding a lost film, including *Sally of the Sawdust* (1925) and *The Sorrows of Satan* (1926), both directed by D. W. Griffith, as well as Frank Capra's *That Certain Thing* (1928). But these, he admitted, were "a drop in the bucket," considering the number of films that are lost to disintegration with each passing year.

Not all film collectors can so confidently be a friend to preservation. For several years, beginning in 1974, the F.B.I. conducted publicized raids against "film pirates"—individuals who are illegally in possession of duplicated prints of copyrighted movies. Among the collectors charged in 1974 was actor Roddy McDowall.

Merle Ray Harlin, who worked as a film editor at Warner Bros., had his collection confiscated in August 1983. It contained the only existing 35mm nitrate prints for the

"Portland Projectionist Saves Film"

In the fall of 1996, two lost American films surfaced in Portland, Oregon. Bill Buffum, a mill worker, who had moonlighted as a projectionist before and after World War II, donated *The Life and Death of Richard III* (1912), one of the first feature-length films produced in the United States, and an early Lon Chaney vehicle, *When Bearcat Went Dry* (1919), to the AFI.

For the last thirty years, Buffum, age seventy-seven, held the two precious titles, which he acquired in trade for his silent film collection. He told reporters that he knew they were a fire hazard, but "these two I felt were worth saving." While he had them Buffum dutifully checked for deterioration. As a result *Richard III* is in near mint condition.

This original nitrate print of *Richard III* is the oldest existing complete American feature film, produced three years before *The Birth of a Nation*. The Joseph H. Kanter Foundation provided funds for a safety negative and several prints to be made. The Kanter Foundation will also help fund national and international screenings of the film.

Frederick Warde as Richard III. *Photos: Courtesy, The American Film Institute.*

"Sought: Nitrate Footage"

Gil O'Gara of Des Moines, Iowa, began collecting silent film in 1973. In the mid-1980s he started actively seeking original nitrate prints. O'Gara knew there was nitrate footage hidden in attics, garages, and barns across America that the archives weren't finding.

"I began advertising and in various ways let it be known that I was seeking silent film. About once a month I get a call from someone who has some silent nitrate. Most of the time it is 'lost' film.

"When we can reach an agreement on price, then I purchase it. When the seller is reluctant to part with the film (most folks think that rarity equals thousands of dollars, when, in reality, nobody is paying much for nitrate), I try to convince them to donate it to an archive and at least get a tax credit.

"Some of my rare film I've donated to the AFI. Some of it I preserved myself because it was beyond what the archives felt was worth spending money on."

For instance, O'Gara bore the burden of transferring a badly disintegrated print of *Christmas Memories* (Universal, 1915) just because he thought "it was a nice film."

O'Gara admits that *Christmas Memories* isn't a classic. "But it is quite representative of the type of fare from that era and in its complete state must have been a beautiful, well-constructed film."

O'Gara has a significant amount of nitrate, including some Vitaphone material, stored in a climate-controlled basement. "Some of the nitrate I'll eventually donate to the archives. It is all a lot of fun, and I think you learn an awful lot about silent film making when you can handle the actual material."

O'Gara is just one of many film collectors who, one film at a time, add to the safekeeping of our cinematic past. As a result the "Gil O'Gara Collection," held by the Library of Congress, contains a number of interesting and rare films that might still be lost if it weren't for this film lover's dedication to preservation.

One of Gil O'Gara's discoveries was forty-three frames from this unidentified comedy. The footage was used as leader on a print of *Christmas Memories* (1915). O'Gara's only other clue to its vintage is that the edge code reads "1917 Kodak."

This piece of brittle, nitrate film—another O'Gara find—is from a Leo Maloney western called *Border Blackbirds* (Pathé, 1926).
Photos: Courtesy, Gil O'Gara.

last two-color Technicolor features Warner Bros. made: *Doctor X* (1932) and *The Mystery of the Wax Museum* (1933). These films were later preserved by the UCLA Film and Television Archive, with support from Turner Entertainment. Another important find in Harlin's stash was the negative for "Lose That Long Face," a musical number cut from the 1954 version of *A Star Is Born*.

More recently some studios have modified their stance on piracy and illegal possession of film. They are now eager to find the best elements for preservation purposes and some collectors have come forward with useful material, often using an archive as an intermediary. Turner Entertainment's Richard May says quite a number of collectors have passed material on to the company through the UCLA Archive.

Films like Buster Keaton's *Sherlock, Jr.* (1924) played at the Vagabond Theatre. Of *Sherlock, Jr.* film historian and preservation advocate Leonard Maltin wrote: "Keaton reached his technical and artistic pinnacle with this brilliant and hilarious story of a hapless projectionist who walks right into the screen and takes part in the imaginary detective drama unfolding."

Silent film expert David Shepard, head of Film Preservation Associates, has supervised many silent film restorations for video and laser release, including the widely acclaimed series *Chaplin: A Legacy of Laughter* and *The Art of Buster Keaton*, which celebrated the 100th anniversary of the comedian's birth in 1995. According to Shepard, the Keaton films may look better on video than they have in theaters during recent decades. "We've been able to make our digital masters mostly from film elements which are closer to the original negatives than are the 35mm exhibition prints. The best of them look astonishing."

At Warner Bros., for example, the studio agreed to collaborate with collectors as much as possible when it was having difficulty finding good material for its restorations of *Rebel Without a Cause* (1955) and *East of Eden* (1955). "It worked to an extent," says Warner vice president Peter Gardiner. The studio offered amnesty, even suggesting that collectors leave their materials anonymously behind a locked door.

In the end, "even with the collectors' cooperation on those two pictures," says Gardiner, the studio chose to reconstruct most of the sound tracks from magnetic prints given to the Library of Congress for copyright purposes.

Collectors are not always philanthropists either. According to James Watters, an executive vice president with Universal:

> We've found that for the most part private collectors have been very helpful. There pretty much has been amnesty because the titles that we're really talking about are titles that are so old they can give us any story in terms of how they got it and we'd probably believe them. . . .
>
> In a lot of cases we've tried to approach private collectors through educational institutions because it seems whenever—and this is not always the case, maybe it's an exception—whenever the name Universal is attached to a piece that we need from a private collector, suddenly there is a very expensive price that goes with this piece.

The Mavericks   One man, one film. —*Frank Capra*

Some films are saved because one individual sticks to one project and gets it done. This is not to say that he did it alone, but rather that *without* him, it might not have be done at all. Three such people are Robert Gitt, Robert Harris, and Ron Haver, and today the preserved versions of *Lost Horizon* (1937), *Spartacus* (1960), and *A Star Is Born* (1954) exist thanks to them.

SAVED: *Lost Horizon*
I think *Lost Horizon* at two hours and five minutes would be ideal. For the remaining seven minutes, only the sound survived and we were unable to find really good still photographs to substitute for the missing picture. Some of this footage just slows things down. However, I was asked to restore the film as nearly as possible to its original state, and this is what I tried to do.   —*Robert R. Gitt*

In 1969 the American Film Institute acquired Columbia Pictures' nitrate vault print of *Lost Horizon*. The AFI staff was delighted to find that it was the 1937 general release version of the film, containing eight minutes of footage that had not been seen for decades. It was not Frank Capra's "complete" *Lost Horizon*, but it was enough to set AFI staffer Bob Gitt off on what would become thirteen years of dedicated detective work. The original negative had decomposed and, in 1973, Gitt began to assemble all of the available copies of the film and use the best parts to construct a master print.

Born in Hanover, Pennsylvania, in 1941, Gitt has been dedicated to film all of his life. His passion for movies combined with his expertise as a technician make him one of the foremost preservationists in the country.

While studying at Dartmouth College, Gitt coordinated the campus film program. He then went to work booking films for the American Film Institute's theater and eventually moved over to the institute's archives in 1973. Gitt has been with the UCLA

Archive since 1977 and is now its preservation officer. He supervises the UCLA preservation program and is personally responsible for major restoration work on a wide variety of films. These include restoring the original Scottish-accented sound track of Orson Welles's *Macbeth* (1948); revitalizing *My Man Godfrey* (1936), the Depression comedy starring Carole Lombard and William Powell, which had fallen into the public domain; and bringing the vibrant Technicolor back to John Ford's spectacular Western *She Wore a Yellow Ribbon* (1949).

Gitt began in earnest to reconstruct the 132-minute version of *Lost Horizon* in 1973, while at the AFI's archives. For thirteen years the project followed him wherever he went. Gitt says he felt as if every time he turned around, *Lost Horizon* was there. He brought the project with him when he moved to the UCLA Film and Television Archive, and there it was finally completed. The story of reclaiming the lost *Lost Horizon* is one of a film—and a man—that wouldn't give up.

Lost Horizon (1936) is based on James Hilton's popular 1933 novel about a storehouse of human knowledge hidden away in the mountains of Tibet in a community called Shangri-La. With a budget of $2 million, it was to be director Frank Capra's poetic masterpiece, and he expected it to be viewed as film "art," superior to the relatively simple movies he had made previously. What actually happened astonished Capra and Columbia Pictures, the studio that financed the film.

In November 1936 *Lost Horizon* played to a very unsympathetic preview audience. The audience laughed at serious scenes. Many people walked out, including Capra, who couldn't bear the audience's response to his film.

Columbia studio head Harry Cohn insisted Capra significantly cut *Lost Horizon*'s running time of well over three hours. Sequences were rearranged, with the new version emphasizing the story's action and downplaying the strong philosophical aspect in Hilton's message. The new running time: 132 minutes.

The second preview at the new length was a surprising success. Harry Cohn was spared a $2 million-dollar disaster and *Lost Horizon* was billed as "Mightiest of All Motion Pictures! Frank Capra's Greatest Production."

Among the important film titles that Bob Gitt has not just "saved" but fully restored are *Hell's Angels* (1930), produced by Howard Hughes and featuring a youthful Jean Harlow, and director Budd Boetticher's semi-autobiographical *The Bullfighter and the Lady* (1951), produced by John Wayne.
Photo: Wendy Rosin Malecki.
Courtesy, UCLA Film and Television Archive.

Ronald Colman is a visitor and a prisoner in Shangri-La, a utopian hideaway in the Himalayas.

Director Frank Capra was eighty-nine years old when Bob Gitt began the restoration of *Lost Horizon* (1937). While there was never any hope of re-creating *Lost Horizon* at Capra's preview length, which was over three hours long, Gitt restored a significant part of the 132-minute version.

Photo: Courtesy, Columbia Pictures. Copyright © 1937 Columbia Pictures Corporation of California Ltd. All Rights Reserved.

The film played a few major cities at 132 minutes and was cut by another 14 minutes for its general release. Though popular, the film did not fully recover its enormous costs until its re-release in the 1940s, when it was cut further to a tight 108 minutes.

There was never any hope of re-creating *Lost Horizon* at Capra's preview length. The 132-minute version, however, seemed an attainable goal. By piecing various prints together, Bob Gitt slowly reconstructed Capra's controversial "masterpiece."

In 1975 a complete 132-minute sound track was supplied by the British Film Institute, which also provided 3 minutes of scenes previously believed lost. And in 1978, Columbia Pictures, the film's copyright holder, found a 16mm French Canadian print with still more missing footage. These two finds gave Gitt a total of 125 minutes' worth of sound and image. He eventually re-created the remaining 7 minutes using freeze-frame images along with still photographs.

Frank Capra was eighty-nine years old when the restoration began. During the course of the project, he saw a "work print"—a copy of the reconstruction in process. Gitt remembers that Capra was pleased to see key scenes back in the film, especially those with the High Lama, the founder of Shangri-La. In the original version, the High Lama had several lengthy speeches about peace and brotherhood. In 1942 these were cut way down for the wartime re-release.

When *Lost Horizon* was originally released, many critics and Capra fans were disappointed because the film was so different from his earlier movies. Capra's audiences expected entertainment, not idealistic philosophy. Screened today, however, *Lost Horizon* transcends the Depression era in which it was made. For many modern viewers, the film has a lasting appeal and effectiveness that is lacking in some of Capra's more topical films.

Thanks to Bob Gitt's careful restoration, all of us have an opportunity to see a more complete version of Frank Capra's dream of Shangri-La once again.

SAVED: *Spartacus*

There are a few films that I remember from my teens that showed me the power of film, that made me want to get into filmmaking. And when I feel one of these films is disappearing, I have to do something about it. It's as simple as that.   *—Robert Harris*

These are the words of the *very* independent film archivist/producer/restorationist Robert Harris. Growing up, Harris was interested in two professions—archaeology and film. The process of reconstructing and preserving motion pictures involves unearthing bits of celluloid instead of shards of pottery. Harris has become an archaeologist in the microcosmic world of film.

He brings some of the romance of the buried past to film preservation. Harris once described cans of film as being "like so many urns of grain in an ancient tomb." His role was to "unlock the gates through which the grains of wheat would fly and grow yet again."

Harris was raised just outside of New York City and studied film at New York University. He began working at Seven Arts Productions when he was fifteen years old and, shortly after college, he formed his own film distribution company.

Harris's introduction to film preservation came in 1975 when he became involved in the restoration of Abel Gance's *Napoleon*. The reconstructed film was released in 1981 and was a commercial success. Harris followed this in 1989 with the highly profitable "director's cut" of *Lawrence of Arabia*, and in 1990 produced *The Grifters* with Martin Scorsese.

Robert Harris's love of movies has made him a strong, opinionated advocate of the films he admires. Following his well-received reconstruction of *Lawrence of Arabia*, Harris tackled *Spartacus* (1960), a film that had a powerful impact on him as a teenager.

Harris says he knows that the Kirk Douglas/Stanley Kubrick Roman epic is not one of the two or three greatest films ever made; however, "It's a damn good film, and it's a film that needed to be restored."

In 1960 *Spartacus* cost Universal Pictures $12 million. Presented in wide-screen Super-Technirama-70mm, the film was the most expensive Universal release to that date. "If you had to redo it today," says Jim Katz, who produced the restoration with Harris, "it would be pushing $100 million."

The film was immensely popular and netted $14,600,000. Nominated for several Oscars, and winning Best Color Cinematography, Best Color Art Direction, and Best Color Costume Design, *Spartacus* was a feast for the eyes.

Its screenwriter, Dalton Trumbo, was one of the Hollywood Ten, imprisoned for contempt of Congress during the House Un-American Activities hunt for Hollywood Communists and blacklisted after his release. Although Trumbo had written screenplays using other names, he was still "officially" blacklisted. Producer/star Kirk Douglas insisted that Trumbo's own name be on the credits, and *Spartacus* marked the writer's true return to the American cinema. Trumbo strongly identified with blacklisted novelist Howard Fast's themes, and his script made the film a serious investigation of the price of freedom.

Harris began *Spartacus's* restoration in October 1989, in partnership with James C. Katz, who had previously headed Universal's Classics Division (1981–1984). Harris quickly realized that the film that had won three Oscars for its color and art direction was a muddy mess.

Robert Harris (left) and Jim Katz (right), who teamed up to produce the restoration of *Spartacus*, are seen here with Harris's son David at the gala opening of their restoration of *My Fair Lady* at the Ziegfeld Theater in New York City (September 1994). Photo: Courtesy, Robert Harris.

Katz and Harris are independents who tackle individual titles using forefront technology. They choose "the biggest and the most difficult"—films they feel passionate about, that desperately need restoration, and that often have technical problems beyond the budgets and expertise of the public archives. They may put years of research into a single title, restoring movies that might not otherwise be saved, and their stunning technical achievements often surpass other restoration efforts.

"What we're doing in the preservation field is unique," says Katz, former head of Universal's Classics Division. "We created the luxury of spending so much energy on one picture. We created

the market. Our high visibility has made the studios more aware of the problems in their vaults; they suddenly realize people want to see these movies.

"We're a boutique operation compared to the institutions that are doing the everyday work. Our high-profile pieces do a lot to raise awareness of the real preservation problems that exist."

Harris and Katz choose films that will draw audiences back to the theaters and will create *profits* for the copyright holders. Their most recent restoration is Alfred Hitchcock's suspense classic *Vertigo*. Katz explains, "Our selection criteria to restore a picture is *much* different from the public archives. The pedigree of the film is important. A costume picture that's timeless . . . the scope of the film . . . the

size of the 'canvas'. . . the universality of the story . . . all this is important.

"*Spartacus* was ideal. It has a cast of thousands. It's a tearjerker. It's an action picture, with a great musical score. And, it has an incredible production history."

When the ravages of time and deterioration have been eliminated, and the sound and picture are restored as close to their original brilliance as possible, the team's hard work and dedication are invisible in the final result. Katz paraphrases critic Janet Maslin's comment about the restoration of *My Fair Lady:* "It's not what you'll see, but what you don't see." That's what makes their restorations so outstanding and such a pleasure for moviegoers to experience.

The original editor's line script—a shot-by-shot record of the film—could not be found. The negative was faded beyond use. The original black-and-white separations had been made but never tested; they turned out to be not only shrunken but improperly made, rendering them extremely difficult to use.

Harris calls Technirama "a bastard child of CinemaScope and VistaVision," and it was this unusual format, which ran 35mm film horizontally, that challenged the preservationist and cost the project a great deal of money.

First Harris had to find a laboratory that could build a printer to convert the horizontal format. Then he discovered he did not have lenses that could handle Technirama's anamorphic qualities. More than one lab attempted to solve the problem, but failed to get both the center and sides of the frame in focus.

"I have the luxury of being as perfect as possible because I am working on one film for a year or a year and a half. I drive the labs crazy," says Harris. In the end, *Spartacus* was put together "grain by grain, frame by frame, rather than reel by reel."

The studio committed nearly $1 million to saving *Spartacus* and in the process made a new 65mm preservation negative. The theatrical re-release of the restored version opened in April 1991 and was followed by a video release.

Harris's restoration of *Spartacus* was also a reconstruction. The film had changed greatly between its final preview in June 1960, when it ran 202 minutes, and when it went into general release at 192 minutes. Many of the original edits were of scenes containing what was perceived by the censors to be graphic violence.

Censors also cut footage known as the "snails and oysters" scene between Lawrence Olivier and Tony Curtis because it suggested a homosexual relationship between the two men. Getting that scene back in the film was not a simple feat. The dialogue track was lost, so the script was re-created by lip-reading the image. Tony Curtis then redubbed his lines in Los Angeles while Anthony Hopkins impersonated the deceased Olivier in a London studio, and Stanley Kubrick "re-directed" the scene—by fax. Mild by today's standards, the once-sensitive footage earned the restored version (197 minutes) only a PG-13 rating.

The backbone of the restoration, says Harris, was the film's original editor, Robert Lawrence, who was responsible for once again giving the film its shape—from memory. "My feeling is that restoration is a highly emotional thing," Lawrence observed. "People want different things restored. But it has to be worth the financial effort [to the studios] or you'll never get it done."

After Harris's experience with the horribly deteriorated negatives of *Lawrence of Arabia* and *Spartacus*, he is an outspoken advocate for preservation of the wide-format, color film. He believes that lack of attention to post-1950s movies "perpetuates the myth that film preservation is dedicated to our remote past, something that belongs more in museums than on theater screens."

Harris urges complete testing of black-and-white separations for *all* films shot in Eastman Color. This would include the full printing of the separations. "No one knows what materials can be produced from protection masters unless they've been printed," says Harris. "Not selectively tested . . . but printed."

In addition to color fading, Harris points out that the 70mm prints from wide-format films were most often made directly from the camera negatives. As a result, these original elements are extremely worn and need immediate protection.

Today, Harris's personal mission is to save the best of the wide-format Eastman Color films. In 1993, he told a Library of Congress hearing:

Make a list of films produced since 1953. Draw a line around 1965. That's the date before which, it's safe to assume, we won't be able to protect anything much longer unless it's already protected.

Take a look at the titles, then dismiss every great film that you'd like to share with your children or grandchildren—or possibly just see again. They aren't going to be there when we want them. It's as simple as that. Either we do something now, and do it right, or let's forget it all. It will soon be just so much junk.

SAVED: *A Star Is Born*

Few are more concerned about preserving cinema's past than [Ron] Haver, once dubbed "the Indiana Jones of film history."

—*Steven Smith,* Los Angeles Times

For preservationists such as Ron Haver, restoring a film to its original glory is an act of love. The work is too hard and the pay too little for there to be any other motivation. The reward is essentially an emotional one—having a movie that was lost live again for a new generation.

When Ron Haver died in 1993 at the age of fifty-four, the field lost one of its most passionate spokesmen. His reconstruction and restoration of the 1954 musical *A Star Is Born* remains a testament to his lifelong love for the movies.

Ron Haver, who truly loved film, organized years of marvelous film programs at the Los Angeles County Museum of Art, including retrospectives on Cary Grant, David O. Selznick, and Ingrid Bergman. His restoration of *A Star Is Born* (1954) came close to fulfilling his lifelong dream to see the film as originally released. *Photo: Courtesy, the Los Angeles County Museum of Art and Ann Calistro.*

In November 1981 the Academy of Motion Picture Arts and Sciences produced and hosted a tribute to lyricist Ira Gershwin. The show closed with a film clip from *A Star Is Born* of Judy Garland singing Gershwin's "The Man That Got Away."

The superior sound system in the Academy theater reproduced all the nuances of this rare stereophonic version, and Garland's emotional rendition made for a thrilling theatrical moment. The audience was as excited as if they were hearing the torchy ballad for the very first time. There was a tremendous ovation.

This reception inspired the Academy Foundation, the division of the Academy that is responsible for education and preservation efforts, to embark on a search for a complete stereophonic version of the film.

The idea was strongly supported by screenwriter Fay Kanin, then the president of the Academy and later chair of the National Film Preservation Board. The recent theatrical success of the newly restored silent French epic, Abel Gance's *Napoleon,* demonstrated that impressive restorations could draw audiences. These "new" versions not only entertained, but effectively advanced the cause of preservation and restoration.

In the case of *A Star Is Born,* restoration meant much more than simply cleaning up the negative of the release version of the film. It meant a full-scale search to find the twenty-seven minutes of film cut by Warner Bros. after the movie previewed in the fall of 1954. With this missing footage, a significant cultural and historical artifact could be re-created more exactly.

The 1954 version of *A Star Is Born* is a noteworthy motion picture for several reasons. It was veteran director George Cukor's first musical and his first color film. It was an early showcase for CinemaScope and stereophonic sound, two important technological innovations of the period.

The movie was also an important "comeback" for superstar Judy Garland, who had been absent from the screen for four years. And, with a final cost of $5,019,770, *A Star Is Born* was one of the most expensive movies made up to that time.

To recoup this astronomical figure, the film would have had to gross twice its budget; at that time, only eight films had grossed over $10 million. Although heralded by the studio as "The Most Anticipated Event in Entertainment History," *A Star Is Born* had a long climb at the box office just to break even.

The film is a lavish remake of a simpler dramatic version of the story released in 1937, with Fredric March and Janet Gaynor. And while Garland's emotional performance and the opulence of color and CinemaScope are part of what eventually made the 1954 version a "cult" classic, they are also elements that made the film somewhat excessive for audiences at that time.

A Star Is Born opened at Hollywood's Pantages Theater on September 26, 1954, with a running time of 182 minutes. Overall, the reviews were good, but even by mid-1950s standards, the film was overly long. In the 1950s a big-city, first-run theater screened a hit picture seven or eight times a day, with a sizable audience for each show. Exhibitors complained that at three hours, *A Star Is Born* cost them critical audience turnover. A shorter running time meant more box-office dollars and, eager for a quicker return on its investment, Warner Bros. trimmed twenty-seven minutes.

This editing was done as economically as possible. Without consulting Cukor, the studio made wholesale cuts, removing two production numbers and fourteen minutes of character development that took place early in the film.

The result, some believed, severely compromised Moss Hart's screenplay and director Cukor's work. Cukor and Judy Garland adamantly refused ever to see the truncated version, and for twenty-nine years audiences saw nothing but the edited release.

A Star Is Born's 1983 reconstruction was conducted by film historian Ron Haver, assisted by the film's production designer, Gene Allen, who was available for consultation during every step of the project. Warner Bros. and the Academy acted as financial backers and Eastman Kodak donated film, freeing money in the budget to restore the stereophonic sound track.

In Haver's detailed account of the project—*"A Star Is Born": The Making of the 1954 Movie and Its 1983 Restoration*—he describes the impact the movie had on him in 1955. "I was sixteen when I first saw *A Star Is Born*, and it was one of my primal movie-going experiences, the kind of epiphanic film that burrowed itself into my subconscious and reverberated there."

He saw the film in San Leandro, California, a small town outside of San Francisco.

Not all restorations are born equal. Ron Haver had a $25,000 budget to animate the still photographs that filled in for missing footage in *A Star Is Born* (1954). Bob Gitt, by contrast, had only $500 available to rephotograph his images for *Lost Horizon*.

The drive-in sequence in *A Star Is Born* is one of several deleted segments that Ron Haver restored to the film. Shot on location at Stan's Drive-in at Sunset and Cahuenga boulevards, it captures a little slice of old Hollywood. Here Judy Garland (as carhop Esther Blodgett) takes an order from Chick Chandler.
Photo: The Academy of Motion Picture Arts and Sciences. Copyright © 1954 Warner Bros. Pictures Inc.

There, the Bal Theatre was newly equipped with CinemaScope and stereophonic sound. When Garland belted out the last line of "Born in a Trunk," the sound was so intense that the theater's crystal chandelier tinkled.

This is not the kind of movie experience one is likely to forget. In fact, young Haver's passion for the film ran so deep that he wrote to Warner Bros. asking if the full-length version he had read about could be seen. His letter was never answered.

Over the years Haver avidly collected stills of all the missing sequences and pursued various leads to track down the missing footage. The odds were against him, however. The trims from prints edited in 1954 had been returned by exhibitors to the studio and destroyed. Sections cut from the negative had also been junked by the studio.

In 1972 Ron Haver was the director of the film program at the Los Angeles County Museum of Art, where he presented a George Cukor retrospective. For the screening of *A Star Is Born,* Haver made a brochure using stills and script excerpts illustrating the missing sequences.

Haver's brochure helped spark interest at Warner Bros. in finding the missing footage. After a search of the Warner holdings in California and New York, a complete sound track of the full-length version was unearthed. "If the complete track existed," Haver wrote, "the complete matching picture must be somewhere within the confines of the Burbank lot."

It was not. For weeks, Haver personally combed every storage space on the lot, including Jack L. Warner's vault, which contained a great deal of film from *A Star Is Born* but none of the missing footage. Haver's hopes were alternately raised and dashed as he exhausted every lead. Finally, he concluded that the missing sequences were truly lost.

His search, however, did uncover almost twenty minutes of usable footage, mainly from the Warner stock footage library where the studio had stored the footage of the exterior scenes. The principals had been carefully edited out so the footage could be cut into future films. In these same cans Haver found the alternative takes for the deleted musical sequences.

Haver had reclaimed a total of nineteen of the twenty-seven minutes. He used still photographs taken on the set during filming to illustrate the remaining time on the full-length sound track. The scenes that relied on still images were given the illusion of movement by rephotographing them with a moving camera.

Haver had also found a pristine, original Technicolor dye-transfer print of the edited version, which was used as the basic footage for the reconstruction. And, just as the restoration was about to be released, a negative of the "Lose That Long Face" number was seized from a collector's illegal hoard. Quickly printed, it was cut into the film to replace Haver's reconstructed version.

A Star Is Born showcased in major cities across the country and in Europe, complete with an intermission, which was part of the original exhibition design. George Cukor believed "neither the human mind nor the human ass can stand three hours of concentration."

On June 30, when the new *A Star Is Born* premiered in New York's nearly six thousand–seat Radio City Music Hall, it was dedicated "to the cause of preserving the world's motion picture heritage." While not every frame of film was restored as Ron Haver had hoped, the 1983 "premiere" version of *A Star Is Born* is the closest modern audiences can come to seeing the complete version of George Cukor's film.

Fay Kanin honored her good friend's memory and spirit in her introductory remarks.

The rebirth of *A Star Is Born* is a testament to the enduring artistry of our colleague and friend George Cukor. For twenty-nine years, this uncompromising artist refused to look at the cut version of his masterpiece. On the night before he was to see this reconstructed version, he died. Tonight's screening has a very special meaning for all of us, for tonight would have been George's eighty-fourth birthday.

Haver supervised the creation of the video version of the new *A Star Is Born,* but was unable to convince Warner Bros. to use a "letterbox" format, which would maintain the elongated CinemaScope aspect ratio. Ironically, he found himself "panning and scanning" (electronically trimming to fit a TV screen) the film he had worked so hard to present in its original form.

He was not unhappy. The video picture is beautiful and the stereo track is outstanding on a superior home system. "Some folks with chandeliers," Haver reflected, "may even manage to recapture my own experience at the Bal Theatre thirty years ago."

Snow White and the Seven Dwarfs was originally filmed in three-color Technicolor, Successive Exposure. Each frame of full-color artwork was photographed three times in succession through blue, red, and green filters onto a single roll of black-and-white film, recording the tonal values of the three primary colors as negative silver images. The difference in tonal values can be seen here with the Queen. When a composite of the three frames is made using filters and an optical printer, the result is full color. (See the Queen in full color on the Cinesite monitor.)

To protect this black-and-white nitrate negative, a Successive Exposure Master Positive was made directly from it using a contact wet-gate printer. From this master positive an internegative on color stock was created, and it was this protection negative that was the starting point for Cinesite in the 1992 digital restoration.

For archival storage, Eastman Color films are inversely protected. The original color negative is photographed through blue, red, and green filters onto three separate rolls of film, creating the yellow, cyan, and magenta separations commonly called a "YCM."

Photo: Copyright © Disney Enterprises, Inc.

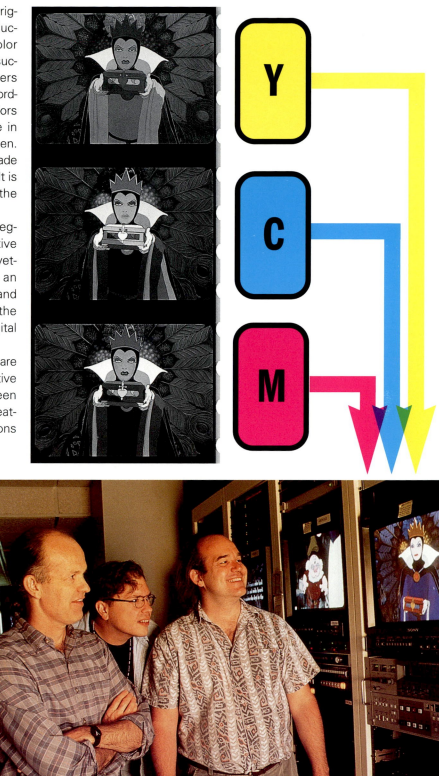

Harrison Ellenshaw, head of Disney's visual effects department, Tim Hauser, and Cinesite creative director Bruno George take a look at a revitalized image of *Snow White*'s Queen. Disney characters.

Photo: Courtesy, Disney Enterprises, Inc., and Cinesite, Inc. Disney characters copyright © Disney Enterprises, Inc. Used by permission of Disney Enterprises, Inc.
Photo copyright © Waldo Bascom.

Distinguished as the first full-length animated feature, *Snow White and the Seven Dwarfs* was voted one of the ten best pictures of 1938 in the annual Film Daily critics poll. Walt Disney won a special Academy Award for the film. Presented by Shirley Temple, it is a unique Oscar—a full-size statuette accompanied by seven miniature ones.

Snow White was one of the first twenty-five films to be named to the National Film Registry. For its 1993 release the film was restored and digitized by Cinesite. The result—Snow White, Doc, Happy, Bashful, and Sneezy, and the rest never looked better.

Photo: Copyright © Disney Enterprises, Inc.

In Walt Disney's *Fantasia* (1940), Hyacinth Hippo and Ben Ali Gator frolic to "Dance of the Hours" by Amilcare Ponchielli. Leopold Stokowski and Disney were awarded special Academy Awards for "their unique achievement in the creation of a new form of visualized music" and "for widening the scope of the motion picture as entertainment and as an art form." Not all critics have praised *Fantasia*; some found it a travesty of classical music, despite its contribution to the world of animation. The film was named to the National Film Registry in 1990.

Photo: Copyright © Disney Enterprises, Inc.

James Stewart and Kim Novak star in *Vertigo* (1958). The suspense classic directed by Alfred Hitchcock was one of the first twenty-five films named to the National Film Registry. In 1995 the badly faded Eastman Color negative and the VistaVision format—which exposed film horizontally two frames at a time, doubling the normal 35mm frame size—presented major restoration challenges for wide-format specialist Robert Harris.

"When color fades, the yellow record is the first to go," says Harris. "All the blacks—the shadow detail—turn blue, and the facial tones turn crustacean." This is what one scene from *Vertigo* looked like before color restoration. Kim Novak's coat *should* be pure white.

Vertigo, after restoration by Harris and his partner Jim Katz on the Universal lot, premiered in October 1996 at the New York Film Festival. Kim Novak and the restoration team then traveled to major American cites, including Los Angeles, San Francisco, Chicago, Boston, and Seattle. The restoration is the first feature to be shown in Super VistaVision 70mm with DTS digital sound.

Arthur Kennedy with Peter O'Toole as T. E. Lawrence in David Lean's epic *Lawrence of Arabia* (1962). It took restoration specialist Robert Harris over eighteen months to restore *Lawrence,* longer than it had taken Lean to make the movie! The results were dazzling, and the restored "director's cut" grossed impressive profits in its theatrical release.

SAVED: *My Fair Lady*

My Fair Lady was an enormous box-office success in 1964, grossing more than $50 million in its first year of release. For its thirtieth anniversary, Robert Harris and James Katz, working with seriously deteriorated materials, restored the film to its original splendor.

"The negative was scratched, the splices were falling apart, and there were no usable main titles," says Harris. Additionally, all of the preservation materials were stored in Van Nuys, California, and had been shaken around in the 1994 earthquake. Katz had to use a crowbar to open the vaults. "It certainly pointed up the need for the geographical diversification of elements," says Harris.

With a budget of $750,000, *My Fair Lady* became the first 65mm format film to be restored using Cinesite's digital magic. Not only was color corrected in the twenty-six title cards, but Cinesite also electronically painted out the large film chip lodged underneath the "J" in Jack Warner's name. Their computer artists were also able to eliminate a scratch that was imbedded in the negative.

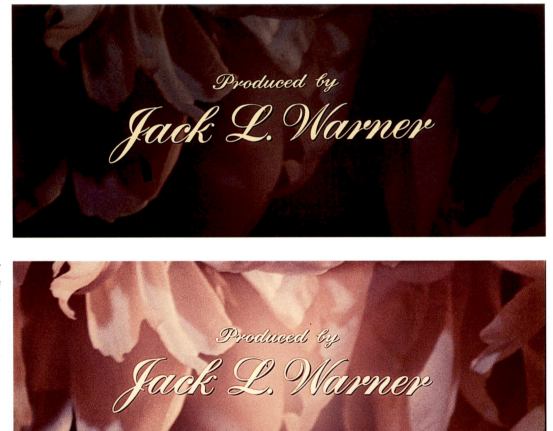

Jack Warner's credit for *My Fair Lady* before Cinesite, Inc., corrected the chip under "Jack."
Photo: Courtesy, Cinesite, Inc. and CBS Inc. Copyright © 1994 CBS Inc. All Rights Reserved.

Jack Warner's credit for *My Fair Lady* after the Cinesite, Inc., correction.
Photo: Courtesy, Cinesite, Inc. and CBS Inc. Copyright © 1994 CBS Inc. All Rights Reserved.

Rex Harrison as Henry Higgins restored to his 1964 crispness.
Photo: Copyright © 1994 CBS Inc. All Rights Reserved.

Audrey Hepburn as Eliza Doolittle back to her original brilliance.
Photo: Copyright © 1994 CBS Inc. All Rights Reserved.

MoMA's Spectacular New Film Preservation Center

The Museum of Modern Art's Celeste Bartos Film Preservation Center, a major new 36,000-square-foot storage and preservation facility for the museum's more than thirteen thousand films plus paper materials, photos, and videotapes, was opened in the summer of 1996. A host of contributors including such names as Rockefeller, Time-Warner, MacArthur, Sony, Gund, and NEA, and all members of the museum's Board of Trustees led by Ms. Bartos provided major funding for the $11.2 million complex a hundred miles from New York City in Hamlin, Pennsylvania.

Made up of two buildings designed to forestall deterioration of the MoMA collection, the center has a staff of six and is not open to the public. Those seeking access to the collection and its databases will continue to use the MoMA offices in Manhattan, to which the center is linked by computer.

"Eventually," says Mary Lea Bandy, "we'll be able to hook up with other archives around the country cataloging descriptive information.

"It's much more than just storage," says Bandy. "It's really preservation, conservation, cataloging, access, and far, far superior handling of the film materials in the cool environment. As we get closer to the new millennium, people want more and more to look back on the twentieth century and examine its history, its social trends, its culture in the largest sense. Once you understand that MoMA is becoming a research institution for the study of the entire twentieth century, then you see that the film collection is one of the museum's most valuable assets."

Part of this valuable asset, five thousand extremely fragile nitrate films dating from 1894 to 1951, are stored in the smaller building in thirty-four individual vaults on slotted, sandwich-type shelves that allow maximum airflow around each can. Surrounded by fire-retardant insulation, maintained at a constant 45°F and 30 percent humidity, these precious films can safely await the funds needed to preserve and restore them.

The main building houses acetate and polyester film and includes vaults for videotapes and photographs. The largest vault has been set aside for original documents, posters, books and periodicals, and production records.

In a humorously whimsical tribute to some of the oldest films in the collection, the Biograph shorts, every room, vault, and closet in the complex has a wall plaque identifying it with a Biograph title. The plaques outside the restrooms read: "Just Like a Woman" and "The Way of Man."

The southwest exposure of the main building of the Celeste Bartos Film Preservation Center.
Photo: Courtesy, The Museum of Modern Art, New York. Copyright © 1996 Paul Warchol for The Museum of Modern Art, New York.

The main building's state-of-the-art workroom.
Photo: Courtesy, The Museum of Modern Art, New York. Copyright © 1996 Paul Warchol for The Museum of Modern Art, New York.

This vault holds the museum's safety-film preservation fine-grain masters.
Photo: Courtesy, The Museum of Modern Art, New York. Copyright © 1996 Paul Warchol for The Museum of Modern Art, New York.

Trouble in Paradise, the 1932 sophisticated comedy directed by Ernst Lubitsch, stars Miriam Hopkins (center) and Herbert Marshall (right).

The film is one of thousands of Hollywood nitrate-era films stored and protected at MoMA's Celeste Bartos Film Preservation Center in Hamlin, Pennsylvania.
Photo: Courtesy, The Museum of Modern Art, New York. Copyright © 1996 The Museum of Modern Art, New York.

Kirk Douglas, who stars as Spartacus—a slave who leads a revolt against the Roman Empire—also served as the film's executive producer. This frame from the film's 1991 restoration shows *Spartacus*'s unusual format, which challenged restorer Robert Harris—widescreen Super-Technirama-70mm. This process ran 35mm film horizontally, eight perforations at a time, creating a frame twice the size of a normal one. An anamorphic lens squeezed the image by 50 percent onto the frame (hence Kirk Douglas's distorted expression). The image was spread out in the printing process, appearing normal when projected. *Photo: Courtesy, MCA Publishing Rights, a Division of MCA Inc. Copyright © Universal City Studios, Inc.*

The misregistration in this frame from *Spartacus* was caused by the misalignment of the three black-and-white separations. Because Harris worked with shrunken separations for much of the restoration, he was constantly correcting for misregistration. Much of the time during the creation of the preservation master, framing had to be reset shot-by-shot. *Photo: Courtesy, MCA Publishing Rights, a Division of MCA Inc. Copyright © Universal City Studios, Inc.*

The difference between the two-color Cinecolor print of *Becky Sharp* and the Technicolor print restored by the UCLA Film and Television Archive is dramatic. *Photos: Courtesy, Alexander Kogan and the UCLA Film and Television Archive. Reprinted with the permission of Films Around The World, Inc., acting for and on behalf of the Fox/Lorber Associates-Classics Associates Joint Venture, and the Regents of the University of California, Los Angeles, California.*

CHAPTER 7

How Films Are Preserved and Restored

Film has a personality, and that personality is self-destructive. The job of the archivist is to anticipate what the film may do—and prevent it.

—*Orson Welles*

In the widest sense, film preservation assures that a movie—like a great painting or sculpture—will continue to exist, as close to its original form as possible.

Each title that is saved has its own unique story and problems. Its salvation may have been the rather straightforward process of preparing a nitrate negative to be copied to safety stock. Or, it may have required long and complicated "detective" work, searching the world's archives in order to fit a decaying masterpiece back together.

The preservationist who is attending the premiere of a newly restored classic, such as *Lawrence of Arabia,* rubs elbows with the rich and famous and basks in the thrills experienced by the audience. The day-to-day business that makes up life in a film archive, however—the nuts and bolts of preservation—is far less glamorous.

Preservation requires painstaking attention to every detail in the life of the film to be saved. Beginning with proper storage, the motion picture preservationist must take the celluloid through a series of long and tedious steps before a finished work is produced that can be considered "preserved."

Mary Lea Bandy sums up the process:

> Preservation is a complex process. It requires great research and planning to locate
> and acquire film materials; inspect and analyze their condition; catalog historical
> and condition data; assemble materials for copying or restoration in labs and
> supervise the various stages of work; provide proper storage, handling, and access;
> and make prints for public viewing. That is what preservation is all about.

Storage: The Foundation of Preservation

Today, it is universally agreed that the foundation of film preservation is proper storage. That means a cold/dry environment for every kind of film—nitrate, acetate, and color stock. If high-quality master materials

If this brittle strip of nitrate film from
A Night of Terrors (1914) had been left in its reel,
the deterioration in this section would have
advanced, spreading to the rest of the film.
Photo: Courtesy, Library of Congress.

of a modern color film are quickly deposited in a state-of-the-art facility, they may be stable for hundreds of years.

"The reason I put storage at the very top of the preservation definition," says Bandy, "is because I truly believe, as do my colleagues, that proper storage and controlled temperatures retard deterioration better than anything else we can do. It really has become our most important goal, because it gives us *time*."

In the last few years information provided by photochemical studies conducted by the Rochester Institute of Technology and Manchester Polytechnic clearly shows that proper storage *is* preservation.

Jan-Christopher Horak concurs:

It gives us a larger window of time to actually make new acetate masters from nitrate materials. . . .

Correct storage means you have to get as cold and as dry as possible. For years, preservationists have been saying "nitrate can't wait." We believed we had, maybe, ten more years to save nitrate film and then it would all be gone. Now we realize that we have much more time than that. Nitrate will stay with us well into the next century . . . if we have proper storage.

Financed by the profits of their contemporary motion pictures, studio-operated archives have invested millions of dollars building cold/dry storage facilities. However, such optimum facilities are expensive to construct and expensive to maintain. Many public archives lack even a hope of ideal storage, and many thousands of films are stored under conditions that will not significantly delay deterioration.

There is some real progress, nevertheless, not only in the preservation of new films, but also in slowing the decomposition of old ones.

In the 1990s George Eastman House launched a fund-raising campaign to upgrade its nitrate vault, and the Museum of Modern Art finished constructing a state-of-the-art facility costing about $12 million, with separate buildings to house safety film and nitrate. MoMA's new cold/dry nitrate facility contains thirty-four vaults capable of maintaining 45°F and 35 percent relative humidity. While it was an expensive undertaking, Mary Lea Bandy estimates that it would cost $800,000 per year to store the museum's massive film collection elsewhere.

The UCLA Film and Television Archive stores its preservation masters in a cold/dry commercial facility. Unfortunately, its film that is waiting to be preserved does not have that luxury. This is housed in old and less-than-ideal facilities in the former Technicolor Building in Hollywood.

Similarly, the Library of Congress's Motion Picture Conservation Center located on Wright-Patterson Air Force Base in Dayton, Ohio, lacks a state-of-the art environment

The central corridor of the Library of Congress's Conservation Center in Dayton, Ohio. Behind each door is an individual vault. Pictured is Film Vault Manager Sam Tyler.
Photo: Courtesy, Library of Congress. Copyright © 1993 Bruce Thomson.

for its enormous collection. The Library took over the air force's abandoned nitrate vaults in the late 1960s, acquiring ready-made storage with a low overhead. The downside is that although they met recommended standards when they were built in the 1940s, today the vaults are below standard. Though they are able to hold a temperature of 52°F, humidity is a problem.

Preparation and duplication of the Library's nitrate is done in Dayton. The Motion Picture Conservation Center generates the protection copies—the safety preservation masters—that are then kept in cold/dry vaults in Landover, Maryland, at a maximum temperature of 35°F with 25 percent relative humidity. Black-and-white masters are maintained at a more economical relative humidity of 45-50 percent and a temperature of 50-55°F.

Until very recently, film was generally stored in what are now known to be less-than-ideal conditions. It was tucked away in humid garages, rural barns, warehouses, and commercial storage facilities. Strangely, some movies that were abominably stored remained in fine condition, while others that had reasonably good care fell apart rapidly.

This point was driven home in 1994 at UCLA's Sixth Annual Festival of Preser-

This frame from the early silent film *The Two Orphans* (Selig-Polyscope, 1911) shows the beginning stages of nitrate deterioration. In 1994 the Wisconsin Center for Film and Theater Research in Madison, Wisconsin, was awarded $7,000 of AFI/NEA grant money to preserve the film.
Photo: Courtesy, UCLA Film and Television Archive.

vation, when several long-lost Fox productions were screened for the first time in decades. Their discovery was totally unexpected—the kind of serendipity every preservationist dreams of.

When a farm employee died some years ago in a remote village in Czechoslovakia, it was discovered that he had had a "secret" past as a traveling motion picture exhibitor. He had kept a considerable number of titles and hidden them under the floor of a chicken coop. There, beneath layers of bird droppings, a treasure trove of Fox films was unearthed. The stash of prints was reclaimed by Czech archivists, who found the films were remarkably intact, despite being subjected to extremes of temperature and humidity.

This hoard of Fox titles helps to fill the significant hole in American film history left when a nitrate fire destroyed the American stockpile of early Fox films in 1936. Among the titles rescued by the Czech Národní Film Archive and showcased at UCLA were *Monte Cristo,* the 1922 version of Dumas's novel starring ingenue Estelle Taylor and silent film great John Gilbert, and a Tom Mix Western, *The Last of the Duanes* (1924).

Hand-in-hand with proper cold/dry storage to retard deterioration goes routine inspection. Once nitrate deterioration begins, it can spread rapidly. The sooner a section of deteriorating film is spotted, the sooner it can be removed from a reel and the less likely it is to contaminate other footage. Also, if a reel can be caught at very early stages of decay it can go to the top of an archive's priority list and have a better chance of being saved.

"Every year, the Museum of Modern Art staff inspects every reel in our vaults," says Mary Lea Bandy. "Any print that shows signs of deteriorating gets first-priority attention."

Not all film deteriorates at the same speed. The chemicals employed when the film was originally processed and the type of film stock used are just as likely to contribute to the disintegration of an older film as improper storage. Also, the degree to which a print or a negative was used directly affects its rate of deterioration.

"All of us have found to our horror that the most popular, most beloved, most successful films often have the worst damage," says Bandy. "A picture that nobody wants to see might be in excellent shape while *The Maltese Falcon,* for example, is a mess."

Duplication: The Need for a Stable Medium

Proper storage and annual inspection extend the life of both nitrate and acetate stock by retarding deterioration, but "saving" a movie that has already started to decay can only be accomplished by transferring the materials onto the most stable contemporary stocks and immediately storing them in as close to ideal conditions as possible.

For many years the term "preservation" was simply synonymous with "duplication." The preservationist's goal was to create a durable copy without significant loss of quality. Today this is still the goal, but the ability to repair, duplicate, and even enhance old images has become increasingly sophisticated and the art of saving a movie now covers a wide range of preservation and restoration techniques.

The primary job in the public archives is still transferring nitrate titles to safety stock, repairing an archival copy, and making a new acetate or polyester master from that. Public archives do not have the money to "restore" fully all of their titles, so "saving" a nitrate title by copying it to safety is their first priority. Just to do that much for one film requires expert labor, takes months to finish, and costs thousands of dollars.

Each archive takes a slightly different approach to duplication, but everybody

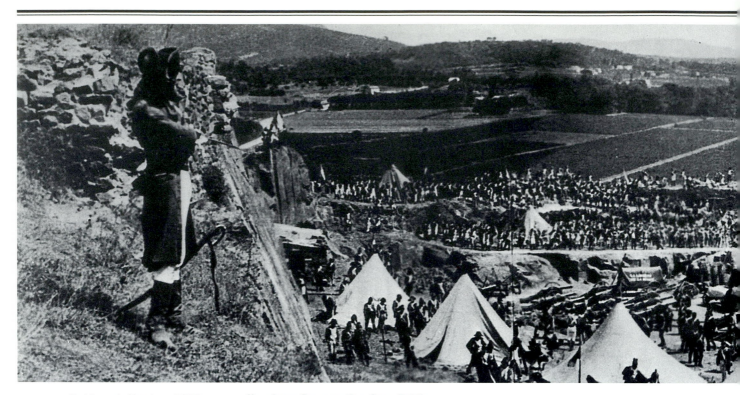

Abel Gance's *Napoleon* (1927).
Photo: Copyright © American Zoetrope and The Film Preserve, Ltd. All Rights Reserved.

Napoleon: Preservation Goes Public

The restoration of Abel Gance's spectacular French silent epic, *Napoleon* (1927), was an enormous box-office success in 1981 and demonstrated that a fifty-four-year-old movie could be a worldwide theatrical event. Playing major cities, *Napoleon* was a phenomenal opening act for the cause of film preservation.

Putting *Napoleon* back together was a twelve-year labor of love headed by British film historian/director/producer Kevin Brownlow. The restoration of Gance's five-hour, color-tinted film included the magnificent, twenty-five-minute "triptych" (three-screen) battle of Italy. The project cost $325,000, and the restored version

follows essentially the same steps. The procedure at the Library of Congress's Motion Picture Conservation Center in Dayton, whose work is primarily the duplication of nitrate, is typical.

About half of the center's work begins with negatives and the other half begins with positive elements. These negatives could be original camera negatives or duplicate negatives. Lacking a negative, preservationists might start with a fine-grain master positive. Any preprint material is generally more desirable than working backward from a projection print.

Library of Congress's Preservation Process: Step by Step

There are four main stages to the Library of Congress's duplication process: a pre-inspection, the preparation of the film to be copied, printing, and the final result—a new preservation master.

To achieve an acceptable preservation master takes dedication, hours and hours of painstaking attention to detail, and even a little tender loving care.

Step 1: Pre-inspection. This initial step is a fast look at each reel of the title to be preserved to evaluate its overall condition. The inspector is looking for gross defects. Pre-inspection is primarily a documentation process, designed to identify potential

was accompanied by a full orchestral score composed and conducted by Carmine Coppola, director Francis Ford Coppola's father.

When the restored *Napoleon* premiered in New York's Radio City Music Hall, its elderly director was too ill to attend. A telephone hook-up was arranged and, at the end of the second night's screening, Gance listened from Paris to the thunderous applause of nearly six thousand *very* satisfied moviegoers.

"They knew that on the other end of the phone was this ninety-year-old direc- tor whose greatest work they'd just seen," remembers restoration expert Robert Harris. "And they raised the roof of Radio City." Eleven months later, Abel Gance died. But thanks to Kevin Brown- low and a host of other film lovers, *Napoleon* lives on.

problems that might arise during the preservation process and to draw conclusions about the best way to approach the project.

An inspection report is written and becomes the preservation plan for the film. It describes the specific work that needs to be done. It notes the different sources or ele- ments with which the preservationist will be working. This pre-inspection stands as a record of a film's condition before work is begun. The film will be inspected again after the preservation work is completed.

Concurrently, the Library consults other archives and the National Center for Film and Video Preservation database to find out whether additional material on the title exists. If another archive has superior elements, attempts are made to borrow them, and this footage is inspected as well.

Looking for alternative source material can slow down the process of preservation considerably. If another archive's material is wanted, an agreement has to be worked out to use it. This inter-archival communication is time-consuming, but it leads to higher- quality final results and cuts down on duplication of effort.

"This cooperation between major archives in America is a relatively new develop- ment," says Ken Weissman, supervisor at the Library of Congress Motion Picture Preser- vation Lab. "It's only seriously taken place in the last couple of years. Before that

Even with improved storage the earliest nitrate-era titles are living on the edge. Emergencies—titles in the beginning or middle stages of deterioration—get priority status at the public archives. This does not mean, however, that there is money to save them. This reel shows the beginnings of advanced deterioration. It can still be saved, but must be copied soon.
Photo: Courtesy, Library of Congress. Copyright © 1993 Bruce Thomson.

everyone was making their choices independently, and I think there was a substantial amount of duplication—especially on the major titles. Everybody wanted to have popular titles in their collection. After all, it is titles like *The Maltese Falcon* that appeal to the general public and generate revenue."

Step 2: Nitrate Film Preparation. Next, a nitrate inspection report is prepared. The film is inspected again—this time, frame by frame. This very detailed documentation is useful to other archivists and is stored in the Library's computer database.

The footage selected to be copied is prepared for the printer. Frame by frame it is repaired. Torn perforations are mended. Old repairs are removed and Mylar tape is used to re-repair the damaged sites. "Old perforation repairs are actually more of a problem than the damage per se," explains Weissman. "In many cases, we can successfully remove those repairs and the damage that's left to the perforations doesn't cause us a problem in printing it."

The center's primary machines are two immersion continuous-contact printers that have been modified to handle as much as 2 percent linear shrinkage. These printers take care of almost all of the Library's projects. A third printer can adjust for up to 3 percent shrinkage—which is considerable. Preservationists rarely come across more.

The film is either cleaned by hand with a film velvet (a very soft velvet cloth that is gently rubbed over both sides of the film) or mechanically, using an ultrasonic film cleaner. Archives that can afford an ultrasonic machine generally prefer to use one. This involves immersing the film in a warm solvent while a generator creates ultrasonic sound waves that pass through the solvent, and literally shake the dirt off of the film.

At the same time the immersed footage is sprayed by jets of solvent, which remove a great deal of surface dirt as well as other substances like projector oil. The most commonly used solvent is methyl chloroform, an ozone-depleting substance that became unavailable January 1, 1996, as an "end use product." Many labs, including that of the Library of Congress, switched to perchloroethylene (the chemical used in wet-gate printing) once their stockpiles of methyl chloroform were depleted.

For a ten-reel feature film, this preparation process can take an experienced nitrate film inspector as little as a day for a sound film (picture and sound track) or as long as several weeks for a reel of a silent title. It all depends on the film's condition.

Step 3: Printing. Now the film is "ready to print" using an immersion continuous-contact printer, in which both the base and the emulsion of the preprint material are immersed in liquid. This creates a copy that is remarkably scratch- and blemish-free, removing between 95 and 100 percent of the base scratches. There is little or nothing a preservationist can do about very deep scratches in the emulsion. Perchloroethylene, the solvent that is used in dry cleaning, is usually the liquid component in immersion printing.

The cement used in old repairs often causes the film's base to shrink. Usually, this shrinkage can be handled by modern printers. The Library of Congress's lab, which has been in operation since 1981, has seven different printers, six of which have different capacities to adjust for varying percentages of film shrinkage.

Some technicians and archivists insist that "step printing"—isolating each frame and rephotographing it—is preferable for the highest quality reproduction. However, continuous-contact printing is less expensive and therefore less time-consuming, freeing staff to get on to more work. It also achieves the important trade-off of a scratch-free copy.

Step 4: A New Protection Master. If the preservationist started with a negative, he or she now has a new master positive from which a duplicate negative can be made.

Ideally the preservationist would now have *two* fine-grain positives: one to provide the basis for the new negative, and a second to be stored as a security backup in case the first fine grain is damaged. Such protection, however, is a luxury and rarely a reality at public archives. Funds simply are not available for backups. In any case, says Weissman, "I'd much rather make one preservation copy of everything, than make two of half of everything and lose the rest."

Once the master positive is made, a duplicate negative can be generated and new prints struck that reflect the repairs done on the original material.

Lastly, a quality-control inspection is made of the new print. The print is okayed and the job is finished. According to Weissman:

> If we started with a negative, we now have a fine-grain master positive. In many cases, that's where we stop. We'd love to have a viewing copy and a projection print on everything we do, but we just don't have that luxury.
>
> If we've made a duplicate negative, then we go one step further and make a print. It's very difficult to analyze a negative for proper quality. You have to look at a print. The whole print!
>
> Then you can say, "This film is preserved."

Preservation Using Multiple Sources Today, preservation isn't always simple "copying." Often, the finished product incorporates pieced-together footage from two or more archival sources. The growing communication and cooperation among archives—and between studios and archives—is making multiple-source preservation more common than ever.

When one or more archives have all the pieces of a film title, restoration can be as simple as putting together a jigsaw puzzle. Other titles, however, may require years of detective work to locate missing or replacement footage.

The least complicated situation is when there are only two sections to match, and the footage is of the same generation. This was the case with the Library of Congress's restoration of the *film noir* classic *The Maltese Falcon* (1941).

In the Library's camera negative of *The Maltese Falcon*, the beginning part of reel two had a tear in it. Half of the scene was torn off for the first three feet. Because it is less noticeable for the audience when footage is replaced at editing points where scenes change, the Library wanted to replace the entire scene.

Inquiries revealed that the Museum of Modern Art had a nitrate-era, fine-grain positive of the film. This print had been made from the Library's original camera negative, and it supplied 99 percent of the needed replacement footage. From their camera negative, the Library printed a new fine-grain master positive that was the same generation as MoMA's. It was then a fairly routine matter to match the contrast levels in the new duplicate negative.

Replacement footage that is spliced into a duplicate negative must match the contrast levels that were in the film when the duplicate negative was made. This matching of contrast levels and exposures (or timing) is controlled in the laboratory and can be a tricky process, especially if four or five different generations of film are being used. The more generations of footage that are involved in a restoration, the more complicated the job of printing a negative.

Ken Weissman compares the Library's restored print of *The Maltese Falcon* (1941) with a 1948
nitrate print.

The Maltese Falcon, the film noir favorite directed by John Huston, was one of the first twenty-five
films named to the National Film Registry in 1989. The film's stars—Sydney Greenstreet, Humphrey Bogart,
Peter Lorre, and Mary Astor—are in the scene above.

Photo: Courtesy, Library of Congress. Copyright © 1993 Bruce Thomson.

Alternative versions of films are common. There are foreign-language versions, **Reconstruction**
or versions edited for television or shortened for re-release on a double bill.
Frequently, films are edited after they are previewed, as was the case in 1937 with Frank
Capra's epic-fantasy *Lost Horizon.*

Sometimes directors themselves cut and recut films. Silent filmmaker D. W. Griffith,
for example, recut and re-edited many of his movies. During the sound era, they were
often issued with an added sound track. When played at sound speed, which is faster
than the speed at which silent films were projected, the running time was additionally
shortened.

When the Museum of Modern Art attempted to restore Griffith's historical epic,
Intolerance (1916), to its full length, the archive found that significant amounts of the
original footage no longer existed. MoMA used still photos in place of lost footage, making the reconstruction less than perfect, as it only approximates the original release version of the film. Unless someday the lost footage is recovered—perhaps in a foreign archive
or in a private collection—*Intolerance* never will be "perfect" again.

Why Are Some Archival Films Incomplete?

- Sometimes a section was removed by the studio to generate replacement footage
- Action sequences (battles, cattle drives, etc.) or establishing shots (sailing into New York Harbor) were lifted out and used as "stock footage" in various other films
- Footage was "borrowed" for use in a compilation film or an educational short
- Footage was damaged and cut out of a reel

We can't prove it, but it's possible that the large sections which were removed from the original material of *Mr. Smith Goes to Washington* were used in another film. We now realize that those educational films we all saw in school showing, for example, the signing of *The Declaration of Independence*, contained feature film footage. —*Ken Weissman*

D. W. Griffith's *Intolerance* (1916) has been meticulously restored by the Museum of Modern Art, using two significant elements from the Library of Congress. Begun in 1981, the restoration took MoMA preservationist Peter Williamson four years and cost $75,000. The restored print has been shown around the world, accompanied by the full orchestral score, conducted by Gillian Anderson.

This monumental film contains several stories, which are thematically related and intercut. The Modern Story, which stars Mae Marsh, was also released as a separate feature, *The Mother and the Law* (1919). The Babylonian Story features a cast of thousands and a remarkable set of breathtaking scale. It was also released as a separate film, *The Fall of Babylon* (1919).

Photos: The Museum of Modern Art/Film Stills Archive.

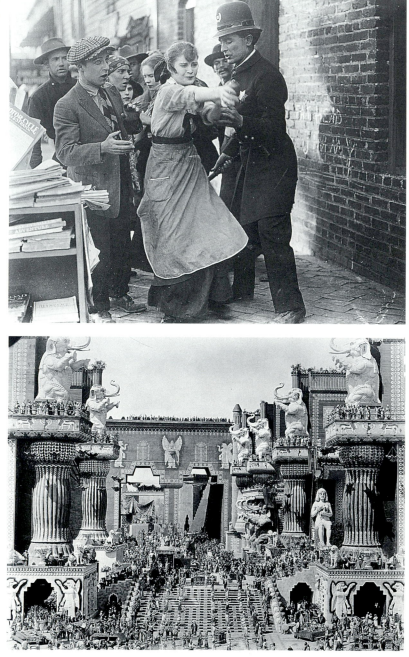

Increasingly "restoration" implies the inclusion of "new" footage: scenes originally shot for the film, but edited out of the final release.

It may be a "director's cut," as was the case with *Lawrence of Arabia* and *A Star Is Born.* Or it might imply the addition of never-before-seen footage, as with Warner Bros.' restoration of *A Streetcar Named Desire* and the studio's anniversary edition of *Woodstock.*

UCLA, MoMA, George Eastman House, and the Library of Congress can only occasionally afford to do lavish restoration projects. The detective work required to reconstruct a masterpiece is too time-consuming and too costly for public archives to do on a routine basis.

Since the early 1980s, however, high-profile restorations like *Napoleon, A Star Is Born,* and *Spartacus* have increased public awareness of the need for preservation. Many of these have been accomplished by independent preservationists and have been backed by the major studios.

Sometimes in cooperation with archives, studios have successfully restored deteriorated motion pictures such as David O. Selznick's classic *Gone With the Wind* (1939). In these cases, marketability and audience satisfaction can, and often do, take precedence over historical accuracy.

To celebrate the fiftieth anniversary of *Gone With the Wind,* Turner Entertainment restored what many still consider America's favorite movie. As of 1989, this monument to Hollywood's heyday had grossed $2 billion—$6.7 billion in inflation-adjusted dollars. The restored version received a gala premiere at Radio City Music Hall, nearly filling the 5,874-seat theater. Five new prints then toured forty-one cities.

Turner, which acquired the rights to the film in 1986, initially intended to restore only the film's impressive main title credit in which *"Gone With the Wind"* literally sweeps across the screen. It was felt that was all that was needed. Seeing this original piece of film, however, made Turner archivists "hungry for the rest of it."

Vice President Richard May, who supervised the restoration, says, "Comparatively speaking, the original [negative] of *Gone With the Wind* was in fine shape. . . . It has been kept the way a fine work of art should be kept."

Despite this safekeeping, it took nearly two years and $250,000 to restore the original, three-strip Technicolor camera negatives, which are stored at George Eastman House, and create a new master positive and duplicate negative.

"It had long been thought that the original negatives had shrunk at different rates," explains Richard May. "In fact the problem was not shrinkage but maladjustment of the prism in the Technicolor camera when [the film] was photographed."

Since Technicolor produces three strips of film, their registration is critical for flawless printing. Without near-perfect alignment of the images, "color fringes" are created when prints are made. In one scene, for example, Clark Gable's tie was a black-and-white check, but it printed as a yellow-cyan and magenta check. In another scene, in which Vivien Leigh and Leslie Howard are seen in profile against a window, the misregistration produced multicolored noses!

Using the old Technicolor printing process, this type of misregistration could be corrected when the matrices (the printing plates) that transferred the dyes to the final

In Turner's preserved *Gone With the Wind* (1939), the Technicolor misregistration was corrected, guaranteeing that Clark Gable's tie was its original black-and-white check and that the profiles of Rand Brooks, Clark Gable, and Leslie Howard had only one nose each.
Photo: Copyright © 1939 Turner Entertainment Co. All Rights Reserved.

release film were manufactured. But as printing processes changed, it became extremely difficult to adjust for the misregistration of the three-strip negatives.

Rather than strictly "restore" David O. Selznick's four-hour masterpiece, Richard May decided to modernize the sound track and color. The sound track was enhanced, eliminating the noise, and a stereo version was created from the monophonic original. In addition, the warm hues of the original three-strip Technicolor were "cooled" down, making the color in the 1989 re-release prints and videos more palatable for contemporary audiences accustomed to the color tonalities of television.

"We will do what we think is a wonderful preservation job, which is completely subjective on our part. And we will hear from a lot of our very good friends from the archives saying, 'We don't agree with that at all. That should have been more blue,'" says Turner Entertainment president Roger Mayer. Indeed, members of the archival community, who traditionally value historic accuracy, would have preserved *Gone With the Wind*'s original Technicolor hues. Still, May feels Turner's restoration destroyed neither the character of David O. Selznick's original aesthetic conceptions nor William Cameron

Menzies's beautiful production design. "I assume that Menzies would probably like it," said May.

Overall, Turner Entertainment takes a very pragmatic stand on restoration. "Somebody made a decision fifty years ago that this should look a certain way, and that somebody isn't here anymore," explained May at the time of *Gone With the Wind*'s fiftieth anniversary reissue. "We have to now take the best example of what they did and make our own."

Turner's new version of *Gone With the Wind* demonstrates that there are varying approaches to film preservation and restoration. One studio or preservationist may choose to re-create (or reassemble) a film, aiming for the moviemaker's original vision or intent. Another may strive to "update" the image or the soundtrack to make it more accessible to contemporary audiences. And yet another may simply try to achieve the very best print possible from the existing elements without employing extensive and expensive restoration.

All of these efforts have been and may be referred to as "preservation" or "restoration." As long as copyright holders retain films, the ultimate choice of exactly how and why to preserve any individual titles will continue to lie with them.

CHAPTER 8

What to Save?

By not preserving film, we're committing cultural suicide. It's madness not to preserve it.
                                        —Martin Scorsese

Eighty percent of the movies produced before 1929 are gone.

Fifty percent of the movies produced before 1950 are gone.

"So, the selection's been made for us," says David Francis, chief of the Library of Congress's Motion Picture, Broadcasting, and Recorded Sound Division. "All we're trying to do now is to preserve what's left."

"What's left" is an overwhelming amount of celluloid, millions and millions of feet of it; there simply aren't enough funds to preserve it all. As a result, every archive must set priorities.

UCLA's Robert Rosen has three standard selection criteria for preservation: *uniqueness and rarity, condition,* and *historical, sociological, and artistic significance.* Sometimes a title falls into only one of these categories, sometimes into all three.

"More than ever before, rarity is a requirement for receiving funds," says Ken Weissman, who in 1994 served on the AFI/NEA grant selection panel.

One of the Library of Congress's current projects that falls into the "rare and unique" category is copying its paper prints to 35mm film. These pioneering motion picture titles dating from 1893 to 1917 were originally transferred onto 16mm in the 1950s, and the image loss in the 16mm copies has prompted the Library to create superior 35mm copies.

Nitrate film preservation continues to be the primary focus for public archives. "We spent a lot of time worrying the nitrate issue and preserving Hollywood films, because we have not had very much choice," explains Paul Spehr, former assistant chief, Motion Picture, Broadcasting, and Recorded Sound Division, Library of Congress. "The nitrate issue is sort of like a tar baby. . . . We have taken on large quantities of it, and we simply cannot abandon it. Without larger resources, we have to stay with it."

George Eastman House has between seven and eight million feet of unprotected nitrate in its vaults, and this remains the archive's first priority. Eastman archivists must also consider their 28mm diacetate material, an unusual film gauge, which includes

Orson Welles was only twenty-six years old when he made his dazzling film debut as director, producer, and star of *Citizen Kane* (1941). *Photo: Copyright © 1941 RKO Pictures, Inc. All Rights Reserved. Used by permission of Turner Entertainment Co.*

American films from the 1910s. These titles *are* unique and, in some cases, they are decomposing more rapidly than the nitrate.

Following rarity and condition, a film's historical significance is taken into account. In the early days of preservation, historical significance was fairly synonymous with *masterpiece,* and the most valued film titles were copied first. Yet, a significant number of the early preservation masters made in the 1970s are unsatisfactory by contemporary standards. So, many of these popular and artistically important films are now being remastered by both public and studio-operated archives. The Library of Congress, for example, has already re-preserved several features directed by Frank Capra.

In the last twenty years preservation techniques and technology have vastly improved—particularly the ability to electronically correct, enhance, rejuvenate, or "mend" damaged images. Just the additional tool of the chemical solvent perchloroethylene, which virtually eliminates scratches and results in far superior preservation, has been a boon to the archives.

Much of the existing preservation material was generated before the archival application of wet-gate and immersion printing, and many scratches in camera negatives were duplicated in the master positives. These then show up in all of the prints. Today, these can be eliminated.

It is reasonable to assume that preservation technology will continue to improve, and this is why archivists argue that nitrate—and acetate—originals ought to be kept as long as they are usable. Ken Weissman explains:

> There's something inherently valuable about the negatives that went through the cameras on the set versus any copies from those negatives. The original artifacts are more valuable simply because they are the original artifacts. So, we want to keep those around as long as possible.
>
> We're doing the best work we can now, but that's not to say that in perhaps ten or twenty years some additional technology won't come around that will

Morocco (1930), directed by Josef von Sternberg, was a popular melodrama starring Gary Cooper and Marlene Dietrich.
Photo: Courtesy, MCA Publishing Rights, a Division of MCA Inc. Copyright © Universal City Studios, Inc.

actually allow us to improve upon that. We saw that graphically with the preservation work done in the 1970s—when most of the preservation programs sprang up. It's not nearly the quality we can do today.

The primary argument against keeping nitrate is a financial one. Ironically, while it is increasingly expensive to store nitrate properly, it is also increasingly expensive to dispose of it in a way that meets environmental and health standards. In 1993 nitrate cost more than forty dollars a pound just to throw away!

Richard Dayton, president of YCM Laboratories, is adamant about keeping nitrate.

I cannot stress too strongly the importance of saving these original elements. . . . It is my understanding that the only element in nitrate film that is harmful to the environment, other than its flammable properties and gases, is possibly the metal reel, plastic core, or container. I'd like to think there might be a new solution to the currently expensive manner in which nitrate film is disposed [of].

While most archivists might like to save the original elements, this nitrate carries with it a hefty annual storage cost. Turner Entertainment's posture, says Roger Mayer, is "selected nitrate backup" and both safety and cost are factors in Turner's decision. Vice President Richard May concurs, "I would lean more toward possibly disposing of [black-and-white]. I definitely would not dispose of any three-strip Technicolor, ever."

"You can't copy everything. And you can't save every possible thing," says Robert Heiber, president of Chace Productions, Inc., whose company has over ten years' experience in restoring motion picture sound tracks for such diverse projects as *Coquette* (1929), *On the Waterfront* (1954), *The Ten Commandments* (1956), and *Rebel Without a Cause* (1955).

Priorities for Preservation Deciding to save a unique or rapidly deteriorating title is a relatively simple matter. These selections are made based on more-or-less objective qualities. However, selecting a title based on historical, sociological, and/or artistic merit involves personal taste and is not so simple.

Here are some of the agreed-upon criteria that go into what Robert Rosen refers to as "judgment calls."

films of historical importance in the development of the art of motion pictures	critically acclaimed award winners
milestones in technology	typical examples of a *genre*
enduringly popular films	works of significant directors
	cultural barometers

Although these guidelines are helpful, clearly no two people are ever going to have identical priorities. One person's masterpiece is somebody else's box-office flop. Committees are frequently used to arrive at a consensus and determine which titles get priority status and receive funding for preservation. As a result of both individual *and* committee decisions, an excellent variety of significant American movies has been preserved. Following are some examples.

Historical Importance: "The Film of Films"

François Truffaut called *Citizen Kane* (1941) "the film of films." Most critics and movie-lovers agree, making *Citizen Kane* a virtually unchallenged masterpiece. And, like a fine cognac, the film has deepened and grown richer with time. When its editor Robert Wise

The Phantom of the Opera
(1925), with Lon Chaney as
the Phantom and Mary
Philbin as the object of his
desire, was preserved by
George Eastman House,
complete with tinted scenes.
The film, which toured extensively, raised important funds
for George Eastman House's
preservation efforts.
*Photo: Courtesy, MCA
Publishing Rights, a Division of
MCA Inc. Copyright ©
Universal City Studios, Inc.*

saw the film's fiftieth anniversary print restored to the big screen, he noted that *Citizen Kane* was ahead of its time and ahead of *our* time.

Orson Welles was twenty-six years old when he made his dazzling film debut as director, producer, co-author, and star of *Citizen Kane*. His innovative uses of narrative construction, lighting, camera, and sound techniques have influenced generations of filmmakers.

The film is very loosely based on the life of publisher William Randolph Hearst, and in 1941, the Hearst newspapers found the movie derogatory and launched an intense campaign against it, successfully reducing the film's initial audience size. Still, *Citizen Kane* received nine Oscar nominations, winning one for Herman J. Mankiewicz and Orson Welles's original screenplay.

In the 1970s *Citizen Kane*'s camera negative was destroyed in a lab fire in New

Robert Wise, seen here on the Paramount Pictures lot, directed such classics as *West Side Story* and *The Sound of Music*. He edited *Citizen Kane* and supervised the film's restoration in 1991. *Photo: Kodak. Courtesy, Robert Wise.*

Jersey, and a true American artifact was lost. Prints made subsequently were struck from a duplicate negative, made from a 1940s-era fine-grain nitrate positive.

As the film's fiftieth anniversary approached, its copyright holder, Turner Entertainment, decided to clean up the duplicate negative and strike new prints for a nationwide re-release. They invited Robert Wise to view Turner's best available print. Wise told company vice president Richard May, "It could stand a lot of improvement." He was promptly enlisted to supervise the film's preservation, and in the process, Wise found himself doing exactly what he had done fifty years earlier.

In 1941 when it came time to print *Citizen Kane,* both Welles and Gregg Toland, the film's cinematographer, were busy with other projects. The printing of America's most impressive film to date thus fell to young Robert Wise and John Swain Robert, who supervised the film's timing.

The Welles/Toland work was not a film to be printed carelessly. Their artistically conceived images relied heavily on extreme contrasts in light and shadow, and their then-radical use of deep-focus photography demanded a crisp reproduction. The twenty-seven-year-old Wise was up to the task, and an older, wiser Wise could guide the restoration.

Welles's innovative sound track—which emphasized overlapping, naturalistic dialogue—cleaned up without much difficulty. Restoration was concentrated on the first three hundred feet of the first reel, which contains the oft-seen footage of the dying Charles Foster Kane whispering "Rosebud." The frequent printing of this sequence for compilation films and clips used in retrospectives had left this section in extremely poor condition.

Unlike some restorations of the 1980s and 1990s, no "missing" footage was added to *Citizen Kane*. No deleted footage, including the rumored "brothel sequence," has yet been found. Even if it were to be found, who would dare to improve on "the film of films"?

Technical Milestones: "The First All-Color American Feature Film"

The film-preservation movement began in earnest with Kevin Brownlow's monumental restoration of *Napoleon*.
    It gained impetus with the reconstruction of the Judy Garland's *A Star Is Born*.
    Now it's come of age with the return of the full-length *Becky Sharp*.
                  —*Kevin Thomas, film critic*, Los Angeles Times

In 1935 director Rouben Mamoulian wrote, "So far the screen had been using a pencil; now it is given a palette with paints." Responsible for the "painting" of the first American feature film shot in the three-strip Technicolor process, *Becky Sharp* (1935), Mamoulian put that palette to good use. Based on the nineteenth-century novel *Vanity Fair* by William Makepeace Thackeray, this landmark film starred Miriam Hopkins as Becky, the self-reliant, self-centered, social-climbing heroine.

When the film was released the *New York Times* reviewer praised Mamoulian's use of full color: "As an experiment, it is a momentous event . . . a gallant and distinguished outpost in an almost uncharted domain."

Mamoulian was known for his artistic experimentation. He was the first director to use a mobile camera in a sound movie and one of the first to use a multi-channel sound track. In *Becky Sharp*, Mamoulian was particularly interested in using color to intensify the drama.

In one of the highlights of the movie, he does just that. On the eve of the battle of Waterloo, a British ball is interrupted by the sound of nearby cannon fire. The wind billows enormous window draperies. The candles are blown out. And, for two minutes, Mamoulian fills the screen with brilliant movement as the fleeing guests are swept from the house like wind-driven leaves.

The women's ball gowns display the full-color spectrum. The soldiers are in red and gold; the orchestra and the other men in black and white. Their colors merge and shift as they flee in the semi-darkness. The scene closes looking down on a red lamp, which throws its scarlet reflection onto a cobblestone street. The crimson-coated soldiers running past seem to blend into a river of red, a harbinger of the bloody battle to come. It is a breathtaking and a successful symbolic use of color.

Until *Becky Sharp*'s 1984 restoration, the film survived only in vastly inferior, two-color prints made by a company called Cinecolor. Memorable scenes, like the ball, were reduced to muddy, imprecise images. The film's sad shape was due in part to the fact

In *Becky Sharp* (1935), Sir Cedric Hardwicke and Miriam Hopkins are at the center of director Rouben Mamoulian's brilliant ballroom sequence.
Photo: Reprinted with the permission of Films Around The World, Inc., acting for and on behalf of the Fox/Lorber Associates-Classics Associates Joint Venture, and the Regents of the University of California, Los Angeles, California.

that it had not been produced by a major studio and had had several copyright owners. Neglected, *Becky Sharp* fell into the public domain.

In 1935 Technicolor's laboratories had generated 448 prints of *Becky Sharp,* none of which could be located when restoration began. Technicolor did still have a ten-minute test reel, originally made for color timing purposes, and this became the standard for the restored color.

Along with this ten-minute reel, UCLA preservationist Bob Gitt had an incomplete 16mm Cinecolor print, a sixty-six-minute 16mm black-and-white negative made for television, and various 35mm negative and positive fragments from the film's original nine reels. Gitt recalled:

As we began the restoration process, we had available to us the following materials: a yellow negative of the full-length version, missing reels four and nine; all nine reels of the cyan negative, but edited to the short sixty-six-minute version; the magenta negative, also edited to the short version, and missing reels two and nine; the nitrate sound track of the edited version, severely shrunken and showing signs of deterioration of reels five through nine, and a portion of reel four. Of the original Technicolor protection positive masters, no reels of the yellow survived; we had the complete cyan master positive of the full-length version to work with, but the magenta master was missing reels five, seven, and nine.

A true jigsaw puzzle, *Becky Sharp* was tediously pieced back together, becoming "the most complex task" Gitt had ever worked on.

As with any three-color Technicolor film, putting *Becky Sharp* back together really meant restoring three films—three separate black-and-white negatives. It took Gitt and Richard Dayton, president of YCM Laboratories, three years to complete it. Aided by a grant from the National Endowment for the Arts, the restoration cost $33,000 and was in part supported by YCM Laboratories.

Gitt and Dayton were able to preserve two-thirds of the footage in full color. Only two of the original three colors survived for the remaining footage, but the color was enhanced in printing to look as good as possible. Though the final result fell short of perfection, it delighted Rouben Mamoulian.

Director Rouben Mamoulian's work is represented on the National Film Registry with his charming and innovative musical *Love Me Tonight* (1932), which stars Jeanette MacDonald and Maurice Chevalier. *Photo: Courtesy, MCA Publishing Rights, a Division of MCA Inc. Copyright © Universal City Studios, Inc.*

Over the years Mamoulian had always cringed whenever *Becky Sharp* was on a festival program. He knew it would be one of the surviving edited Cinecolor prints. Finally, he asked that the film not be shown at all. When the elderly director saw the restored version in 1984, it was an unexpected joy. The color was exactly as he remembered it. After fifty years in shadow his images were restored to their former glory. For Mamoulian it was as though, through some medical miracle, his crippled child had walked once more.

Enduring Popularity: "A Global Audience of One Billion Viewers!"

According to *The Guinness Book of World Records*, the most viewed film of all time is *The Wizard of Oz* (1939). Worldwide, it boasts an audience of over one billion people.

The Wizard of Oz was directed by Victor Fleming and stars a sixteen-year-old singing sensation, Judy Garland. It was not a financial success when it was originally released,

In 1989 Turner Entertainment, the copyright holder of *The Wizard of Oz* (1939), revitalized the film for its fiftieth anniversary. Here, the Tin Woodman (Jack Haley) explains some of the problems of a metallic life to Dorothy (Judy Garland), the Scarecrow (Ray Bolger), and Toto too.
Photo: Copyright © 1939 Turner Entertainment Co. All Rights Reserved.

in part because of its excessive, $2.7 million cost. Now considered an enduring classic, it has long since made its money back.

Its popularity was greatly enhanced when CBS began annual television broadcasts of it in 1956. With the advent of home video, it quickly became a best-seller, and even *before* its fiftieth anniversary restoration, fans had purchased more than a million copies.

The film's charms are many—its innovative use of color (the Kansas scenes are sepia-toned, while the Oz scenes are in Technicolor), a memorable musical score including Harold Arlen and E. Y. Harburg's "Over the Rainbow," and a flawless cast. Judy Garland won an Oscar for her outstanding juvenile performance as Dorothy Gale, which cemented her career as a serious actress.

In 1989 the film's copyright holder, Turner Entertainment, remastered *The Wizard of Oz* to celebrate its golden anniversary. The opening and closing scenes were restored to their original sepia tone, and a mint-condition Technicolor print was digitally transferred onto videotape, providing a new master for the videocassette.

For the celebration, Turner re-released the film in theaters, where it did so-so business, drawing significant audiences only in major cities. The video release, however, had an initial shipment of two million units, an unprecedented number for a title that had been available for years, and was a phenomenal success.

Not only was it the first *true* Technicolor version of *The Wizard of Oz* available on video, but it also contained an element of marketing magic—previously unreleased footage. Turner had not added footage to the film nor created a "director's cut." The bonus was seventeen supplementary minutes added after the movie, of great interest to Oz aficionados. These include Buddy Ebsen, who was originally cast as the Tin Woodman and later replaced by Jack Haley, singing "If I Only Had a Heart," plus an extended specialty dance that had been cut from the Scarecrow's (Ray Bolger's) lively "If I Only Had a Brain" number, which was directed by Busby Berkeley.

In addition, "The Jitterbug," a musical number featuring Dorothy and her three Oz friends, is ingeniously reconstructed. Cut from the film prior to its original release, the much-sought-after sequence was destroyed years ago in a studio fire. The sound track survived, however, and for the restoration home-movie footage shot on the set was combined with still images to replace the missing visuals.

The Critically Acclaimed: "The Negative That Almost Got Away"

Few films have garnered more praise than *Lawrence of Arabia* (1962). Archer Winston of the *New York Post* called it "one of the all-time great films," and then added, "There may never have been in film history a movie which so deftly combines an epic grandeur of scene and action with surpassingly fine and subtle details of character."

The movie was nominated for ten Academy Awards. It won seven, including Best Picture, and also received eight British Academy Awards and Golden Globe Awards. Produced by Sam Spiegel and directed by David Lean, *Lawrence of Arabia* featured an international cast. It was released by Columbia Pictures.

After the film's initial release, Columbia retained the original camera negative and was under the mistaken impression that the picture was intact. The studio believed that the original camera negative, as well as the protection elements (including the black-and-white separations) had never been touched, and that complete sound tracks existed.

When Robert Harris approached the studio about restoring the film, he was told, "There shouldn't really be a problem." Nothing could have been further from the truth.

As it turned out, the 65mm negative *had* been edited, not once but twice, and was extremely fragile. The original mixing elements for the sound track (music, dialogue, and effects)—some 600,000 feet of it—had been junked in 1975. Also gone were the film's continuity sheets, which listed the key numbers of each scene in proper order. As a result, Harris had no written guidelines for the reconstruction.

Harris, his co-producer Jim Painten, and his assistant Joanne Lawson spent over eighteen months restoring *Lawrence*. Even with advice from David Lean and the film's editor Anne Coates, the preservation took longer than it had taken Lean to make the movie!

Harris's biggest single challenge was locating the footage needed to re-create the film's original release length. *Lawrence of Arabia* had premiered at 222 minutes, the same length as *Gone With the Wind*. Both Spiegel and Lean felt it was too long, and, pressured by Columbia to get the movie into distribution, they hurriedly deleted 20 minutes. The 1971 re-release was cut by another 15 minutes, and Columbia's camera negative reflected a version somewhere between the two. Before Harris was finished, he had dug through literally tons of material to reclaim the missing 35 minutes.

More challenges awaited him when he attempted to re-record the film's sound track. The original four-track would not run. The oxide kept flaking off and clogging the playback heads. Harris finally used fourth-generation sound track elements to make a new, fifth-generation track.

Dialogue had to be redubbed. The film's stars—Peter O'Toole, Alec Guinness, Arthur Kennedy, and Anthony Quinn—came to the rescue and generously worked for "scale" (an actor's minimum wage)—or less. Actor Charles Gray impersonated Jack Hawkins, who died in 1973.

The newly recorded dialogue had to be electronically altered so the actors would sound as they did in 1962. Peter O'Toole, the bulk of whose career followed his spectacular performance as T. E. Lawrence, wryly commented when he was redubbing, "Now I know how to read the lines."

When at last the time came to print the preservation master positive, Harris was faced with a self-destructing negative. "All of the splices started opening, the perforations began failing, and the negative surface started cracking up. . . . We were down to the final weeks of life of the negative." Less than thirty years old, the negative lived barely long enough for Harris to finish the preservation master.

The theatrical release of the restored film was a huge success. During the first five months, it grossed $6.5 million—more than ten times the $600,000 Columbia had invested in the restoration. Now labeled the "director's cut," the "new" *Lawrence of Arabia* runs 217 minutes and includes one extended scene that David Lean reluctantly left out of the original. Lean also trimmed a few scenes he felt in retrospect were too long.

For anyone who has seen *Lawrence of Arabia* on the big screen, the experience is indeed unforgettable. For Robert Harris, who had always felt it was the finest film ever made, getting *Lawrence of Arabia* back on the big screen, complete and in proper form, was an honor: "To me, today, the opportunity to see *Lawrence* properly projected on an epic-sized screen is worth everything that went into its restoration. To know that it is preserved for future generations gives me the greatest of pleasures. Ultimately, for anyone who truly loves film, to view *Lawrence of Arabia* is a humbling as well as an exhilarating experience."

Genre Classics

Some titles, in addition to being excellent films in their own right, are outstanding examples of a type—their *genre*. Paramount Pictures' *To Each His Own* (1946) is just that: a fine example of what used to be known as a "woman's picture" or a "weepie." In 1946 the film was so successful as a tear-jerker that theater owners actually complained to its director, Mitchell Leisen. Audiences were crying so hard at the end of the picture they could not see their way out of the theater!

The film's star, Olivia de Havilland, won the 1946 Best Actress Oscar for her distinctive characterization of an unwed mother who sacrifices her happiness for that of her illegitimate son. De Havilland dominates the two-hour-and-two-minute film as she matures from a vivacious and romantic World War I–era girl to a middle-aged "old maid."

The preservation of *To Each His Own* represents a successful joint project between a public archive, UCLA, and a copyright holder, in this case, Universal Pictures/MCA.

Most of the restoration of the film was made possible by a print that had been donated by Paramount to UCLA in the early 1970s. It was the studio's old nitrate projection copy and was filled with splices and scratches.

Olivia de Havilland is greeted by Bill Goodwin in one of the happier moments in *To Each His Own* (1946).
When MCA/Universal bought the Paramount library (1928–1948) and licensed it to television, MCA copied the films to acetate and destroyed the nitrate negatives. Today the best preservation elements available to restore a Paramount Picture from this period, like *To Each His Own*, are often the nitrate studio prints housed at the UCLA Film and Television Archive.
Photo: Courtesy, MCA Publishing Rights, a Division of MCA Inc. Copyright © Universal City Studios, Inc.

"Unlike many of the prints that we received from Paramount that were in beautiful, like-new condition, this one was pretty worn," says Bob Gitt. "I suspect it had been frequently shown to young aspiring actresses because Olivia de Havilland had won an Academy Award for her performance."

Surprisingly, UCLA's old, beat-up studio print became Bob Gitt's most valuable preservation element and was used to re-record the sound. Despite its condition, the print proved invaluable because all the other surviving material, both the sound and the picture, which Universal had owned since the 1950s, had begun to deteriorate.

This preservation material contained flare, flicker, and mottling in many parts of the image. Noises of all kinds—rustling, thumps, and hissing sounds—were also built into portions of the sound track.

At the last stage of the restoration, Universal obtained an Italian print. Dubbed in Italian, the sound track was useless, and the print itself was somewhat milky and grayish-looking. Its overall condition, however, was much better than the studio print, because it lacked splices and scratches. In the end, the Italian print filled in where the UCLA and deteriorated Universal elements were in the worst condition. Gitt explains:

> In a couple of cases, a particular shot in the film had problems in all three sources. The Universal material might have a mottled image at the beginning, then be perfect for the remainder; the UCLA nitrate print might have scratches, splices, and missing frames here and there throughout the shot; and the Italian print, in addition to having poorer overall photographic quality, might have some splices too. In a case like this, we would have to cut back and forth, back and forth during the shot among all three sources. Normally, we try to avoid doing this because there may be visible changes in the positioning or the quality of the picture which will be apparent to the audience. But circumstances force you to do the best you can with what you have.

When Gitt was finished with his "jigsaw puzzle," it contained hundreds of splices. "I'm very happy to say we got the film back together again," says Gitt. And when the print of his beautifully preserved *To Each His Own* was showcased at UCLA's Fifth Annual Festival of Preservation in 1993, a new generation of viewers was still dabbing their eyes as the lights came up.

Great Directors

Many film scholars believe the director is ultimately responsible for the success or failure of a film. The "*auteur* theory" holds that from film to film a director's "touch" or signature can be recognized. From this point of view, saving *every* film in a director's body of work has become a preservation goal. It is as important to safeguard lesser-known films such as John Ford's *Rio Grande* (1950), Orson Welles's *Macbeth* (1948), or Frank Capra's *Broadway Bill* (1934) as it is to safeguard the well-known classics.

Auteurists find a director's failures just as interesting as his or her successes. They want to study both Josef von Sternberg's box-office success *Morocco* (1930) *and* his box-office flop *The Devil Is a Woman* (1935). Of the latter it has been said that the film could be projected upside down and backwards and make as much sense as it does projected properly.

Director Frank Capra's films, many of which were extremely popular when originally released, are works that today interest both scholars and modern audiences. The Library of Congress chose one of Capra's best-loved films, *Mr. Smith Goes to Washington* (1939), as their first big restoration project.

Mr. Smith Goes to Washington, released in 1939, remains a pinnacle in Capra's career and in Jimmy Stewart's. Stewart's portrayal of Jefferson Smith, an amateur politician who turns the U.S. Senate upside down, solidified his career as a romantic leading man and won him an Oscar nomination.

In 1939 the film received mixed reviews. *Daily Variety* called it "the most vital and stirring drama of contemporary American life yet told in film." Another critic, however, complained that Capra portrayed the Senate as "the biggest aggregation of nincompoops on record!"

The restoration of *Mr. Smith Goes to Washington* began in late 1989, took the Library three years to complete, and cost close to $100,000. It was funded in part by the David and Lucile Packard Foundation.

"We chose *Mr. Smith* because the negative was in dire straits," explains lab chief Ken Weissman. "In retrospect, *Smith* may not have been an excellent choice to start with because of severe problems associated with it. We might have been better served starting with a little bit simpler project."

The Library's Motion Picture Conservation Center in Dayton, Ohio, found there

Claude Rains watches James Stewart's apparent downfall during his filibuster in the Senate, in *Mr. Smith Goes to Washington* (1939).

In 1939 some critics felt that Frank Capra's film showed the virtues of the democratic system, while others felt it made a laughingstock of the Senate.

Photo: Courtesy, Columbia Pictures. Copyright © 1939 Columbia Pictures Corporation. All Rights Reserved.

was little first-rate material existing for the film. Surprisingly, there were only two nitrate elements still available. One was the original negative, which was full of replacement footage, and the other was a heavily used release print made from the European negative that the Library borrowed from Britain's National Film Archive.

The Library also had two fine-grain safety positives that came from Columbia Pictures, and a not-particularly-good safety negative made in the early 1960s. The main problem with this negative was a technical one. It had a very low contrast-level, making it difficult to generate a good print. In the past, no one had wanted to work with this problematic negative, so it had not been used much and was in very good condition.

On the other hand, the camera negative, which was the Library's only nitrate source material, was missing significant pieces of the film. It had been used extensively in the 1960s and 1970s to make new prints for theaters and television, as well as for generating videocassette masters. As a result, it was badly torn up, and one section of about three hundred feet had been replaced with safety negative film that had been blown up from a 16mm print. There were also a couple of short sections completely missing from the negative. So, the not-particularly-good duplicate negative came in handy and was used to replace the blown-up three-hundred-foot section.

As with Capra's *Lost Horizon,* there had been more than one release version of *Mr. Smith Goes to Washington.* This gave an added twist to the re-creation. The center staff documented five versions, all of different lengths, to determine which version should be restored. They elected to go with the longest (roughly 129 ½ minutes), which they believed was the original and popular release version.

The process began with an evaluation of the nitrate negative. A restoration script was prepared, indicating all of the sections in the original negative that needed to be replaced. Other archives were searched for superior copies of the missing and battered parts. Replacement footage was gathered, assembled, analyzed, and compared with the negative material. The best available elements were used to reconstruct the film and became the basis for the new master positive.

In 1939 *Mr. Smith Goes to Washington*'s preview in Washington, D.C., was a spectacular social event. Among the four thousand guests were forty-five U.S. senators. In November 1993 a slightly less spectacular, but no less satisfying premiere was held for the reconstructed version, although the representatives and senators scheduled to attend the screening at the Freer Gallery were kept away by a congressional night session.

"In my mind, that didn't detract from the screening," says Ken Weissman, who supervised the restoration. "The film got a really marvelous reception, and I was very pleased with its overall look."

Subsequently, Sony Pictures Entertainment released the Library's restored version on video, and thanks to the efforts of the Library of Congress, the general public can once again enjoy one of America's best-loved movies in its entirety.

Cultural Barometers

[UCLA's] preservation philosophy is based on the conviction that "average" films should be preserved alongside acknowledged masterpieces—that it is not the archivist's job to second-guess history.

—*Robert Rosen*

Archivists like Robert Rosen approach selection with a certain humility. "One of those anti-Communist movies of the '50s may be terrible, but of great importance sociologically," says Rosen. *I Was a Communist for the FBI* (1951), for example, may bring chuckles when played today, but at the time it was a serious, documentary-style exposé of the Communist menace.

"Remember, tastes change," Rosen points out. "Grade 'B' movies of the '30s and '40s were hardly regarded as art objects, yet by the '70s and '80s many of them had become *films noir.*"

An example is *Detour* (1945), a very cheap B-picture that runs a scant sixty-nine minutes, which was quickly lost to memory after its initial release. But when French critics and filmmakers proclaimed its director, Edgar G. Ulmer, an *auteur, Detour* and other Ulmer films became the subject of serious study. Today it is included on the National Film Registry as a national treasure.

Detour (1945), directed by German-born Edgar G. Ulmer, features Tom Neal as New York nightclub pianist who hitchhikes to Los Angeles. Filmed on a shoestring budget, *Detour* is a surprisingly expressive and bleak *film noir.*

An era's "typical" movies are often cultural barometers. These were not "great works" when they were released and have not necessarily become "great works." They are, however, accurate reflections of their time, exhibiting the essential characteristics of the society that made them.

This category takes in everything from testaments to the Jazz Age like Cecil B. DeMille's *The Godless Girl* (1928) to World War II propaganda, such as *This Is the Army* (1943) starring Ronald Reagan, both of which have been preserved by the UCLA Film and Television Archive.

Today a fourth consideration for preservation might be added to Robert Rosen's "rarity, condition, and significance" criteria. It is a title's ability to generate revenue.

For the public archives, screenings and licensing can significantly augment tight budgets. In 1992 UCLA raised a healthy percentage of its entire operating budget through the licensing of footage from the Hearst Metrotone News Collection. Likewise, George Eastman House preserved and distributed *Princess Tam-Tam* (1935), starring cabaret star Josephine Baker, and netted approximately $20,000 for other projects.

For the studios the marketability of a preserved title plays an important part in determining their priorities. Sony Pictures Entertainment, for example, has worked with the various public archives to establish a standardized method for the planning and prioritizing of their library. For Sony, this means integrating market demands with the opinions and goals of the preservation community.

What Price Preservation?   The mother's milk of all of this is money and the hope for preservation lies in getting adequate funds for the job.
                                                                                               —Fay Kanin

Most of the footage in public archives was given to them for safekeeping by the producers of the films. Archives actively solicited material and producers were often happy to give it to them. In these cases, the copyright owners retained the rights to use and exhibit the titles on deposit and the archives provided storage and preservation.

"Archives do insist on the right to make preservation materials which will be the property of the archives; depositors may have one-time access to these preservation materials," says Mary Lea Bandy.

What does it cost to make these preservation materials? The laboratory figures range tremendously. Black-and-white nitrate, for example, might cost as little as a dollar or two per foot to copy onto safety. In 1993 the price of transferring color stock was about five dollars per foot.

One minute equals ninety feet of film. At 1993 prices, just to duplicate a ninety-minute, black-and-white, silent film costs between $15,000 and $20,000. The costs for a sound film climb closer to $30,000. A color title of the same length ranges between $30,000 and $40,000. In 1991 Eastman House estimated their cost for restoring Cecil B. DeMille's *Northwest Mounted Police* (1940), shot in three-strip Technicolor, at $45,000.

George Stevens, Jr., of the AFI put it well:

> The difficult part is money. . . . We felt that this nitrate rescue effort would be done and then everything would be fine. The lesson was that this was merely the beginning, that there are more and more and more films being made, and the fact that they are made on safety film did not guarantee their survival. Loss and carelessness and inattention put them in jeopardy.

In the period between 1980 and 1992, the price of duplicating a ninety-minute, black-and-white silent film increased from an average cost of $3,234 to $13,730. Simultaneously, funding for film preservation—especially government funding—severely decreased. By 1995, in adjusted dollars, federal funding for the AFI/NEA and Library of Congress programs was half its 1980 level.

Maureen O'Hara and Roddy McDowall in *How Green Was My Valley* (1941).

Produced by Darryl F. Zanuck at Twentieth Century–Fox, *How Green Was My Valley* is one of the many significant films on UCLA's priority list. Directed by John Ford, the movie is a beautifully filmed story of life among the families of Welsh coal miners as seen through the eyes of a boy (Roddy McDowall). It won five Academy Awards, including the Oscar for Best Picture of 1941. In 1990 it was named to the National Film Registry.
Photo: Copyright © 1941 Twentieth Century–Fox Film Corporation. All Rights Reserved.

UCLA's Priority List

How Green Was My Valley is one of the ninety-two titles from the 1930s and the 1940s on UCLA's priority list for saving feature films in their collection. Since most of these are available on videocassette and are still regularly seen on television, what exactly is endangered?

It is the *best* material or the *complete* material that UCLA strives to protect. Here is a sampling of the others, which includes some that are considered the most important titles of the era.

Alexander's Ragtime Band (1939)—Tyrone Power and Alice Faye

The Awful Truth (1937)—Cary Grant and Irene Dunne

Beau Geste (1939)—Gary Cooper and Ray Milland

Counsellor-at-Law (1933)—John Barrymore

The Dark Mirror (1946)—Olivia de Havilland and Lew Ayres

Destry Rides Again (1939)—James Stewart and Marlene Dietrich

The Major and the Minor (1942)—Ray Milland and Ginger Rogers

My Darling Clementine (1946)—Henry Fonda and Linda Darnell

Road to Morocco (1942) and *Road to Singapore* (1940)—Bing Crosby, Bob Hope, and Dorothy Lamour

Wee Willie Winkie (1937)—Shirley Temple and Victor McLaglen

In 1980 the AFI/NEA grants (not including matching funds) totaled $514,215. These funds then supported the duplication of the equivalent of 159 black-and-white silent features. In 1992 the AFI/NEA awards dropped to $355,600, which funded the equivalent of fewer than twenty-six features.

"Unfortunately, political and budget constraints are such that the $150,000 annual grant we got from the National Endowment for the Arts beginning in 1980 has been whittled down to $97,000 this year," said UCLA's Robert Gitt in 1993. "Over the same period, print and development costs have quadrupled."

Despite the dwindling purchasing power of the NEA grants, when the AFI/NEA Grant Program for film preservation was discontinued in 1995, the archival community expressed a range of emotion from concern to outrage.

Although the AFI/NEA avenue no longer exists, film preservationists can apply to NEA and direct grants have been awarded, beginning in 1995. The funding pool definitely shrank, however, and now archives must choose between applying for funds to support programming and funds to support preservation.

MoMA, UCLA, and George Eastman House are heavily dependent on outside fund-raising to meet their budgets. For example, MoMA's 1994 budget for duplication was $350,000. These funds came entirely from endowment income, grants, and donations.

Jan-Christopher Horak, formerly the senior curator at George Eastman House, explained the archive's fund-raising strategy before the loss of the NEA as a source of grant money:

> We have several different sources for film preservation: government funds (our yearly budget from NEA is $100,000), foundations, and individuals. In our fund-raising, we accept very small donations. Anything.
>
> I travel and show preservation work from the archive, and people come up and say they'd like to give a little bit of money. We have a couple of retirees who will give us a thousand dollars. Some give five hundred. One gentleman put us into his will.
>
> And now the AMC Preservation Festival is a source. We had hoped for some big-league gifts from various Hollywood people, which never came through. The donations were all very small ones made by the people who watch AMC. And it still amounted to $220,000. This means that each of the major archives got about $40,000, which is not a lot of money, but it certainly allowed us to preserve a couple of films.

Susan Dalton, director of Preservation and Archival Projects at the AFI's National Center for Film and Video Preservation, agrees. When her program received an unsolicited, individual contribution of $450, it made a difference. "It made a difference of $450," says Dalton, "and we greatly appreciated it."

UCLA has similar sources for funding. Half of the archive's operating budget, which included a staff of thirty-four employees in 1995, comes from the University of California. Until 1995 federal funding for preservation came to about $100,000 annually from the AFI/NEA Grant Program, with another $30,000 from the NEA Media Arts program for public programming. UCLA also has a $255,000 grant from the National Endowment for the Humanities to preserve 1930s footage from the Hearst Newsreel Collection— the first such film preservation grant in the history of that agency.

Additionally, support from the David and Lucile Packard Foundation, the Stan-ford Theatre Foundation, Hugh Hefner, the Cecil B. DeMille Trust, the Mary Pickford Foundation, and the Harold Lloyd Estate has saved many films.

In 1994 UCLA funded over 90 percent of its laboratory expenses ($292,694) from outside sources, and their Annual Festival of Preservation programs indicate that the number of smaller donors grows every year. These include foundations, corporations, and individuals who give $50,000 to save a color film or $15,000 to save a black-and-white title.

The David and Lucile Packard Foundation: To the Rescue!

The David and Lucile Packard Foundation has been a substantial friend to film preservation, providing over $2 million worth of support to the UCLA Film and Television Archive alone. One recent grant has gone to preserve seven classic titles including an early film starring Cary Grant, the Harold Lloyd feature *Safety Last,* and Lloyd short subjects. Another grant for $100,000 funds the full restoration of *Joan of Arc* (1948), starring Ingrid Bergman.

At the Library of Congress money from the foundation funds the salaries of eight staff members and has made it possible for the Conservation Center to add a second shift of technicians to transfer nitrate to safety stock.

With private funding of this magnitude the future of film preservation in the United States has a rosier outlook. And it all started when Bob Epstein took David Packard to Los Angeles's Vagabond Theatre to see a UCLA-preserved print.

Universal has restored *Frankenstein* (1931) to its original release length, including all the censors' cuts made in subsequent reissues. One of the restored sequences, well known among film buffs, depicts the Monster innocently throwing a little girl into a lake. The studio also added some scenes which had previously not been seen by American audiences.
Photo: Courtesy, MCA Publishing Rights, a Division of MCA Inc. Copyright © Universal City Studios, Inc.

What's Past Is Prologue   I'm sure it's difficult for anyone to understand why the studios haven't funded preservation before.

—Mary Lea Bandy

As funding has become an escalating problem the public archives have looked to the copyright holders for help. Turner Entertainment, at least, is ambivalent about paying for preservation of archival material. President Roger Mayer explains:

> I'd like to comment that I think we should pay when it is our obligation to do so. But in all cases where nitrate was contributed, whether to the Library [of Congress] or other archives, we were asked to contribute and we volunteered to do so. And the archive wanted to spend the money to hold onto it and preserve it because they felt it was a public-spirited thing to do, or an artistic thing to do, or whatever their reasons were. And we said, "Okay, if you feel that way, fine." And now you're coming back and saying, "Whoops, we forgot to ask you to pay for it."
>
> . . . And in effect this would be an additional tax on us, and we certainly should discuss it and we certainly should consider the pros and cons of it. But I don't think any of us are ready to say to you, "You're absolutely right, we should pay for it." I don't think we're ready to do that yet.

The challenging question at this moment in the history of film is who preserves what and who pays for it. The Library of Congress's 1994 recommendation to Congress to establish a federally chartered foundation to raise private funds for preservation portends a new era for the safekeeping and salvation of our movie heritage.

Looking to the future, Robert Rosen warns that the responsibility is ours alone:

> Future generations living five hundred or a thousand years from now will look back at the first hundred years of motion pictures, the time when it all began and will be eager to study and restudy, to view and re-view every aspect of what we created. They will shake their heads in disbelief wondering why "they" allowed so much to be lost. The archive must convey with all of the conviction we can that the "they" are us.

Our Movie Heritage:

The Second Hundred Years

The moving picture is not so much the art form as the language of the twentieth century. Future generations will wonder why so little of such a marvelously accessible and appealing record was ever preserved or seriously studied by the strangely transparent and otherwise exuberant society that produced it all.

—*Dr. James H. Billington, Librarian of Congress*

In general the American public still thinks of film as neither art nor language but as *product;* a commodity to be viewed, rented, or bought. If we are to save our movie heritage, this point of view must change. As David Francis of the Library of Congress believes, "The film archive must be moved from the world of commerce to the realm of the fine arts."

The move that has taken place is a shift in attitude on the part of the commercial owners of movies. They are now much more convinced of their product's long-lasting value—in artistic, cultural, *and* economic terms.

Simultaneously, the public's awareness is shifting too. The creation of the National Film Preservation Board and the National Film Registry keeps the subject of film preservation in the news. And, in 1993 and 1994, reports on the government-sponsored hearings on film preservation did much to increase public understanding of the crisis at hand.

Film Preservation in America: Conclusions and Recommendations

In 1983 Frank Hodsoll, then chairman of the National Endowment for the Arts, wrote: "I was appalled to learn that half the theatrical films produced before 1952 have already been irretrievably lost due to decay and neglect. Under present conditions, most of the remaining half will not survive this century."

Today there is much more reason to hope that a very high percentage of what is left will make it into the twenty-first century and onto more stable media.

In June 1993 the results of the Library of Congress's definitive study on the state of film preservation was published in four volumes. These included the report itself; transcripts of the hearings held in Los Angeles and Washington, D.C.; and compiled statements, papers, and reports submitted to the Library about the current state of film preservation.

"I don't really like the term *film preservation*. It's a misnomer. . . . *Moving picture preservation* is much better, because you can't preserve film; it's too unstable."
—Ron Haver
Photo: The Academy of Motion Picture Arts and Sciences.

The hearings before the Librarian and a panel of selected National Film Preservation Board members featured testimony by top representatives from the preservation field. The report summarizes a massive amount of information and presents a variety of opinions on how to deal with current preservation problems.

One of the important distinctions the report makes is between the two categories of films that need to be saved: those that have market value and are exploitable by their copyright holders, and those that are "orphans," lacking either clear copyright holders or commercial potential to pay for their continued preservation.

This second category contains the majority of films at risk: newsreels, independent productions, avant-garde films, documentaries, silent films on which the copyright has expired, and even a few Hollywood-produced sound films that have fallen into the public domain.

Titles in the public domain are those whose copyrights have expired and have not been renewed. Generally, copyrights cannot be renewed beyond seventy-five years. For example, by the end of 1997, films created and distributed before 1923 will be in the public domain. Recent law has simplified copyrights and any film registered after 1963 has one seventy-five-year term of ownership.

Preserving Films to Be Seen
In a can it is nothing. A film is preserved when it is on a screen in front of an audience with people reacting to it.
—Henri Langlois

Paul Spehr, now retired from the Library of Congress, says the Library's original goal was not to preserve film for posterity, but to make it *accessible*.

Robert Rosen points out that the UCLA Archive is committed to making films available *and* to presenting them—in the finest quality original form.

Mary Lea Bandy agrees. "We want films to be preserved so that they may be *seen*."

In *It's a Wonderful Life* (1946) an angel named Clarence (Henry Travers) helps George Bailey (James Stewart) understand that every man's life is important.

It's a Wonderful Life, one of the first fifty films named to the National Film Registry, is an example of a film in the public domain that reaped benefits because it was easily available to the general public. At the 1993 hearings, Greg Luce, a member of the Committee for Film Preservation and Public Access, pointed out:

> After its copyright lapsed in 1975, [*It's a Wonderful Life*] was basically rediscovered by the public. It's only been since that time that it's become established as an all-time American film classic.
>
> Now, this isn't to say that every forgotten film from the golden age of Hollywood is going to become a classic someday, but it certainly shows that widespread availability encourages widespread appreciation which results in a work becoming more permanently ingrained into our culture. We believe the entire film history of Hollywood deserves this consideration.

To study film, to write film history, or even just to enjoy the films of the past, one must be able to see the films. Yet many film scholars who made submissions and testified for the Library's 1993 study felt strongly that publicly funded restorations were not available to the public. Somewhere along the way access to archival films has become a minor goal.

Even public domain titles can be withheld from the general public through contractual restrictions. A donor can give a title to an archive and restrict its use in perpetuity. As long as this system exists, taxpayer money is being used to preserve films that may remain unavailable—forever.

One outspoken "public availability" group is the Committee for Film Preservation and Public Access, whose members include preservationist Robert Harris and film historians Gregory Luce, Leonard Maltin, and Anthony Slide. In a 1993 submission to the Library of Congress, this group presented a very convincing case for "films that might as well be lost." Using the films of Gary Cooper as an example, the committee pointed out the difficulties a scholar would have in viewing Cooper's complete body of work.

Children of Divorce (1927), one of Cooper's silent films, which starred Clara Bow,
    is preserved, yet this preserved copy has never been publicly screened.
The Spoilers (1930) has never aired on television due to restriction concerning
    the Rex Beach story on which it is based, and Paramount, the copyright
    holder, has not distributed the film.
One Sunday Afternoon (1933) has been preserved with public funds, is in the
    public domain, yet is virtually never shown.

The committee submits that Paramount Pictures, which donated prints of these titles to the Library of Congress in 1971, does not have the titles in distribution, yet "refuses to allow access to films like these by specialized distributors."

An added frustration is that two very significant Cooper titles, *Meet John Doe* (1941) and *For Whom the Bell Tolls* (1943), have been restored to their full lengths by public funds, but are currently still unavailable on video in their restored versions. Still another important Cooper title, *Saratoga Trunk* (1943), is restricted because of a "limited license" to the Edna Ferber novel on which the film is based.

"Gary Cooper is one of the great film stars in the history of American cinema," concludes the committee. "Yet seven of his major films are currently unavailable to the pub-

A Farewell to Arms (1932), starring Gary Cooper and Helen Hayes, fell into public domain and is easily accessible to scholars and the public. This is not the case for at least five of Cooper's films, which are preserved but are rarely, if ever, seen.

lic in their original or restored form. At the same time, all are being preserved by archives that receive Federal funds."

Since this testimony both *One Sunday Afternoon* and *Saratoga Trunk* have shown on Turner Classic Movies, and AMC aired *For Whom the Bell Tolls* as part of its second Preservation Festival. This clearly demonstrates how valuable these cable stations are to public access of classic films.

Additionally, as a result of the Library of Congress study, Paramount Pictures has agreed to discuss with the Library the possibility of releasing selected public domain pictures from the terms of their original deposit agreement, making them accessible for viewing.

Gradually archival titles are also appearing on videocassette and on laser disk. The Library of Congress's Video Collection (distributed by Smithsonian Video), for example, focuses on previously unavailable American silent titles and the origins of American film genres. The collection contains features by pioneer women directors and important examples of African-American cinema.

Likewise restorations from materials held by George Eastman House have been digitized and are available on video as well as on laser disk produced by Lumivision. These classic titles include *The Phantom of the Opera, The Lost World,* and *The Last of the Mohicans.*

The Committee for Film Preservation and Public Access eloquently states: "Just as a falling tree makes no sound if no one is around to hear it, preserving a film makes no sense if no one is allowed to see it."

Archives can be frustrating gatekeepers for many individuals who would like copies of films or just want to view a film for scholarly purposes. It can appear, says the Library of Congress report, that the archives are "perversely saving films for a posterity that never quite arrives."

The reasons are not always perverse, however; sometimes they are strictly economic,

---

"Serve the Public—Or Die"

Brian O'Doherty of the National Endowment for the Arts eloquently summarized the state of film preservation for the Library of Congress 1993 hearings:

I was present . . . the first time that studio heads and the heads of nonprofit archives got together and sat at the same table.

. . . Elton Rule looked at the studio people and said, "I do not know how much you are interested in film preservation; I think the only form of preservation you know about is self-preservation."

That was in 1985. We have come a long way. . . .

A field once industriously submerged in the twilight of isolated repairs has emerged into unaccustomed sunlight. A great consciousness raising has taken place even as the fiscal landscape has become more parched and inhospitable. . . .

Some 10 million in tax dollars has gone to nitrate preservation from the Endowment over the past twenty years—the longest and most sustained investment outside that of [the Library of Congress]. . . .

What has the public got in return? . . .

Who profits from preservation? Studios locating lost originals legally or illegally held? Specialized exhibitors? Home videos of tasty morsels? The usual ranks of admirable scholars? Well, where is the public?

Let us follow the preservation cycle for a moment. A lost silent film . . . is found in a remote archive in New Zealand. It is returned, restored, transferred to acetate. It is catalogued, databased, written about. Surprisingly, the acetate is stricken with vinegar syndrome.

It is treated, retransferred, remastered. What happens to it then?

It is preserved as if in aspic. For whom? . . .

For no matter how bright the radiant screen of their memory, the public will not long support preservation without seeing its results. . . .

I am aware of what Eastman House does with silent film and live musical accompaniment. But the lack of a sophisticated exhibition habit in our great national museum of many archives is, I choose my word carefully, a disaster. . . .

I think that question of who is served is becoming increasingly important for our agency. . . .

Serve the public or die.

Most of us have grown up with the written word being our main form of communication. We are opening a new frontier where visual communications will become increasingly more important. The tools we offer provide ways to expand that vocabulary.

—Ed Jones, president of Cinesite

At present, there is still no reasonably priced electronic solution for preservation. The cost of restoring Disney's *Snow White and the Seven Dwarfs* using the Kodak Cineon digital film system was estimated at several million dollars.

It is very expensive to capture the nearly five million pixels held in one frame of film without significant loss of detail. Even the digital standard for high-definition television captures less than half of the visual information on 35mm film.

When an economically viable electronic preservation method does develop, archivists may be cautious about embracing it. They have had too much experience with the rapid obsolescence of a multitude of electronic technologies, particularly video formats.

Despite the promises of new technologies, Richard Dayton of YCM Laboratories believes that "even though the current buzzwords are digital, HDTV, and so forth, long-term preservation of film images and sound is still safer on film."

as was the case with the 1932 version of *Tess of the Storm Country*. One single nitrate print of this Janet Gaynor vehicle survived into the 1970s. At that time UCLA only had the funds to create a safety negative, not a positive print as well. The result was that the film was unavailable for screening until funds were provided by the AFI/NEA Film Preservation Grant Program and the Louis B. Mayer Foundation.

In 1996 UCLA proudly presented Janet Gaynor's *Tess of the Storm Country* at its eighth annual Festival of Preservation. It had taken two decades to make the step from preservation negative to an accessible, and beautiful, 35mm projection print.

Some archives such as the Library of Congress, the UCLA Film and Television Archive, and the University of Wisconsin (which holds prints of classic Warner Bros., RKO, and Monogram titles), welcome scholars. Others do not—or do not have the option to do so.

Access is frequently complicated by agreements made with the donor at the time of the gift. Currently, it is possible for a donor to restrict or refuse access to a film even after the copyright has expired. "We have people who own copyrights who do not want even a single viewing by a scholar in a lonely booth," says Librarian Billington.

Why? Studios and producers fear piracy—that others will exploit their product. Just as in the early days, when filmmakers chopped up old films to prevent illegal copies, today some would like to lock them up and throw away the key. Each new innovation in film duplication adds to this fear.

Redefining Film Preservation: A National Plan
I think the public archives would like nothing better than to concentrate their efforts on the orphans.

—David Francis, Library of Congress

Part II of the Library's report outlines a "national plan," addressing the concerns and questions raised in the initial study. Completed in August 1994, the plan stresses that preservationists are facing a crisis in saving our film heritage and suggests the role the federal government can play.

The recommendations of the Librarian of Congress list the basic steps necessary to save America's films *and* make them accessible to the public. The plan stresses the importance of proper storage as preservation's best ally, addresses the problems of how to provide access to preserved films, and advocates establishing a federally chartered foundation to raise desperately needed funds.

One suggestion for saving America's movies is through a division of labor and expenses.

> Copyrighted titles would be cared for by their owners, freeing the public monies to handle the orphans—"the motion pictures of cultural and historical importance that will not survive without public intervention."
> Storage costs would be shared—in other words, the studios would pick up some of the bill for copyrighted materials held in public archives.
> International ties would be strengthened—particularly in the attempts to repatriate "lost" American films held exclusively in foreign archives.

One of the most promising recommendations of the report, the suggestion to create a National Film Preservation Foundation, became law in October 1996. Federally chartered, the foundation is a public-private partnership designed to raise private funds, which are then matched with limited federal funds. The foundation can award grants to film archives, historical societies, and other nonprofit institutions for the preservation of non-Hollywood films and "orphans."

Director and film preservation advocate Martin Scorsese made the first donation to the foundation and praised the Library of Congress's new role in the field:

> This Foundation will be the ideal mechanism to ensure the long-term preservation of America's film heritage, especially that portion not controlled by commercial interests. Serving as the much-needed central fund-raising repository and administrator of public and private sectors (studios, film producers and artists,

I Am a Fugitive from a Chain Gang (1932) a Warner Bros. release, was added to the National Film Registry in 1991. For its day, the film was a shocking exposé of abuses in the criminal justice system. Paul Muni, who starred as a slightly fictionalized version of convict Robert Burns, won an Academy Award nomination for Best Actor.

Fugitive is one of twenty-seven feature films traveling on the National Film Registry Tour, designed to bring preserved movies to the general public. Turner Entertainment, which owns many of the titles on the National Film Registry, has provided extremely valuable promotional support for the tour via its cable network Turner Classic Movies.
Photo: Copyright © 1932 Turner Entertainment Co. All Rights Reserved.

archives, the education community, and others) in a cooperative effort to preserve American film. I, along with other film artists, plan to support the work of this Foundation actively and enthusiastically.

The report also announced the 1995 National Film Registry Tour, designed to raise public awareness about film preservation and provide theatrical access to preserved and restored titles. The tour celebrates American filmmaking and enables audiences to experience significant American films as they are intended to be seen—good-quality prints projected in public theaters.

The tour presents the preservation work of many organizations and a wide variety of Registry titles, including twenty-seven features and selected shorts. Among these are *Raging Bull* (1980), *Gigi* (1958), *The Treasure of the Sierra Madre* (1948), *Sunrise* (1927), and the Bugs Bunny classic *What's Opera, Doc?* (1957).

Beginning in October 1995 the Library embarked on its goal to bring the tour to at least one city in each of the fifty states. A sold-out crowd of 1,300 greeted actor James Earl Jones, the Librarian of Congress, Dr. James Billington, and chair of the National Film Preservation Board, Fay Kanin, on the tour's opening night in Madison, Wisconsin.

The first history was written in the hope of preserving from decay the memory of what men have been.
  The great guerrilla war of our time is the battle between memory and forgetting.
  With "forgetting" comes *the great lie, the official story, war, despair, repetition, ignorance, folly, purposelessness.*
  "Memory" as Wordsworth says—"that inward eye"—is the crown jewel of our evolution.
  Preserve it.
  Preserve your dream life.
  Preserve film.   *—Oliver Stone*

In 1995 theatrically projected movies celebrated their one-hundredth anniversary.

As the second hundred years of motion pictures begins, there is still much to salvage from the first one hundred. The signs are favorable that a significant percentage of this vital part of American history will be saved and that the films produced in the twenty-first century will be cared for with a new consciousness for the future.

The actual results are up to all of us.

What's past is prologue. . . .

Henry B. Walthall and Lillian Gish in D. W. Griffith's masterpiece *The Birth of a Nation* (1915).
Photo: The Museum of Modern Art/Film Stills Archive.

You Can Help

Every contribution, no matter how small, helps the cause of film preservation. *You* can help! To make a personal donation to one of the public archives, here are their addresses:

George Eastman House
Attention: Development Department/Film Preservation
900 East Avenue
Rochester, NY 14607

The Library of Congress
Attention: David Francis, Chief
M/B/RS Division
Washington, DC 20540-4800

Make checks payable to: National Film Press Foundation

The Museum of Modern Art
Attention: Chief Curator Mary Lea Bandy
Department of Film and Video
11 West 53rd St.
New York, NY 10019

The UCLA Film and Television Archive
302 E. Melnitz
405 Hilgard Avenue
Los Angeles, CA 90024-1323

Make checks payable to: The UCLA Foundation (Account #5350)

Glossary

There [are] many, many different terms for very valuable material.
—*Peter Gardiner, vice president, Warner Bros.*

Even after half a century of film preservation, the terms used in the field are often not used consistently with a commonalty of meaning. This is in part because the film preservation movement in the United States did not grow in any centralized way. Disparate efforts across the country in the archives, in the laboratories, and at the studios have resulted in a variety of terms, often used in a variety of ways.

A common vocabulary is still in the making, but the Library of Congress's 1993 report on film preservation led to some of the following definitions.

Acetate. See under **base**.

Active preservation. See under **preservation**.

Answer print. See under **prints**.

Base. The transparent support layer of the film, typically made of celluloid. The common base materials are 1) *cellulose nitrate,* or nitrate; 2) *cellulose triacetate,* or acetate; and 3) *polyester.*

Nitrate's chemical composition destabilizes over time. It has a tendency to shrink, to give off acids that destroy both the base and the emulsion, and to become highly flammable at relatively low temperatures.

The expression *safety* film refers to both *acetate* and *polyester.* Polyester, which has been available since the mid-1950s, is not commonly used; laboratories prefer not to work with this base because it requires its own splicing techniques. *Acetate* is now known to suffer from decomposition—commonly called "the vinegar syndrome" because of the odor it gives off.

The vinegar syndrome was first noted in the late 1940s, but has only recently become a major archival concern.

Camera negative. The negative that was in the camera when the movie was shot. In the best of all possible worlds, this negative would only have been used to generate an *interpositive,* not to generate prints.

At the Library of Congress, preservationists actually start with a camera negative about one-third of the time.

Even these negatives, however, are not always intact or complete. They are not always in good condition and often contain replacement footage, particularly if the original negative was used to generate prints. It is not at all unusual to find a negative that consists of various generations and may even include very poor quality safety duplicate material or footage blown up from 16mm copies.

Conservation. Conservation requires no physical copying, only the decision to treat film material with greater care because of its perceived use as a future preservation source.

Digitally remastered. This term often appears on videocassettes and usually refers to re-recorded and digitized sound.

Duplicate ("dupe") negative. The negative made from an *interpositive,* used to generate prints and to protect the camera negative from wear and tear.

Archivists sometimes have to create a duplicate negative to protect the earliest surviving generation of a film, as well as to strike *viewing prints.* Especially in the case of silent films, many of which have survived only through *projection prints,* archivists must work backwards to create a negative from the print.

Elements. "We try to start from material that is most complete, in the best condition and, ideally, the lowest generation."   *—Ken Weissman*

1st Generation	*Camera negative*	
2d Generation	*Fine-grain master positive*	*Projection print*
	Lavender positive	
3d Generation	*Duplicate negative*	
4th Generation	*Projection print*	

Each time film is duplicated quality is lost in the duplicate. The sharpness of the image starts to soften. For this reason, a preservationist wants to work with the earliest generation of a film as a basis for a new preservation master.

Also, when a negative is used time and time again, damage increases, the image loses sharpness, and all of this is passed on to any new prints.

Emulsion. Light-sensitive layer that carries the image. It is the dull side of the film, consisting primarily of gelatin and silver salts.

Film. A thin flexible strip of transparent *base* material coated with a light-sensitive *emulsion* on which photographic images are registered when taking motion pictures. All motion picture film consists of these two primary layers, base and emulsion, with a binder to hold them together.

Fine-grain master positive. Also known as the *interpositive.* A positive version of a film made specifically for duplication purposes. It is considered an intermediate element. The interpositive becomes the main preservation element and is used to make duplicate negatives.

In a fine-grain positive the overall contrast between the blacks and whites is very low. The whites become medium grays and the blacks become dark grays.

Nothing in the frame is truly black or white. Instead, the fine grain presents a "flat" range of grays.

Because prints increase in contrast with each duplication, the negative made from this flat positive will contain the true blacks and whites of the original camera negative.

A safety fine-grain positive of a nitrate title is found occasionally, although not often. This most likely would be a preservation copy dating from the 1960s or 1970s.

First generation. See **camera negative**.

Fourth generation. See **nitrate-era 35mm print**.

Immersion continuous-contact printer. Printer in which both the film to be copied (the preprint material) and the raw stock (the unexposed safety film) are immersed in a solvent solution and moved past a light source. The new copy is printed continuously in direct contact with the preprint material. This type of duplication is a very rapid process, and continuous-contact printers are preferred in production laboratories. Anywhere from one hundred to one thousand feet of film can be exposed per minute.

Interpositive. See **fine-grain master positive**.

Lavender positive. Nitrate-era positive made on *negative* stock. These prints had an extremely low contrast level, and were used as preservation masters. The base's bluish tint resulted in the name lavender.

Liquid-gate printer. See **wet-gate printer**.

Nitrate. See under **base**.

Nitrate-era 35mm print. A print made on nitrate stock.

This is a less desirable place to begin preservation work if the print was made from a duplicate negative. It is still preferable to a safety print or a 16mm copy. If the print was made from the original camera negative, as *second-generation* material, it might be the best element available.

One-light print. See under **prints**.

Passive preservation. See under **preservation**.

Polyester. See under **base**.

Preprint materials. These include *camera negatives, fine-grain master positives,* and *duplicate negatives.* These are the various elements from which viewing prints are made.

Preservation. "Preservation means taking the original materials and reproducing them onto the most stable possible format so that they can be passed on to future generations."
—Robert Rosen

While preservation can be thought of as any effort to keep a film in a viewable form, most archivists consider a film preserved only when it is both 1) viewable in its original format with its full visual and aural values retained, and 2) protected for the future by *preprint* material through which subsequent viewing copies can be created.

Active preservation. Preparation and duplication of film; simply the physical copying of existing material.

Passive preservation. Storage and inspection of a title.

Prints. Not all archives and laboratories agree on how to handle printing from preservation masters, and no universal standards exist. At present, the Library of Congress is the only public archive running its own laboratory. The following terms and procedures are based on their current practices:

Answer print. Also known as *first-trial print.* The first print from a final, cut negative. It is the first time sound and picture are married in a print. This print is suitable for a scholar to use on a flatbed (editing table) for research purposes, but not "perfect" enough to project in a theater.

Following the first answer print, *timing* adjustments usually have to be made. Commercial laboratories may print several versions before they show the client the official answer print.

One-light print. Whether the Library is printing from a nitrate positive or a duplicate negative, in most cases a one-light exposure is made onto the new safety generation. This is a single, overall exposure for the film. It is much less labor-intensive than scene-for-scene timing, and therefore less expensive. Scene-for-scene timing is often not necessary, because the previous generation has already been timed.

The one-light method does not work well for silent films, which make up about 60 percent of the Library's preservation work. These must be timed scene for scene. In silent negatives, the footage with titles may differ dramatically in exposure from the footage with pictures.

Studio-produced sound-era films need fewer adjustments. They were shot under much more controlled lighting situations.

When starting from a *fine-grain master positive* or a repaired nitrate print, a one-light print is even more acceptable because positives and prints are timed when they are made.

Projection print. Also known as *viewing print* or *release print.* The highest quality print. Before the lab is satisfied with the quality, it has probably printed one or two *answer prints.*

Reference print. A second *answer print* (with timing corrections) might become a reference print. The Library of Congress screens reference prints in its own theater, The Mary Pickford, and loans them to other archives for screenings.

Timing. The scene-to-scene adjustment of the exposure of film to produce the best-looking print. The Library's answer prints are electronically timed, using a video analyzer. This results in a print that is fairly close to projection quality.

The goal is to achieve a consistent tonal balance from shot to shot and from scene to scene. Preservation work can require specialized timing when different generations of film must be matched.

Projection print. See under **prints**.

Reconstruction. Sometimes used interchangeably with *restoration,* reconstruction implies that pieces from various sources had to be fitted together.

"At MoMA the *reconstruction* of a film means to re-create the original release version of the country of origin. This means restoring parts that had been cut out or damaged or destroyed in one way or another, taking out parts that were added and changed in later versions, and trying to reassemble the pieces of image and sound (if it's a sound title) to the version that originally appeared in the theaters. That is also the standard of the International Film Archives Association (FIAF)."

—Mary Lea Bandy

Reference print. See under **prints**.

Restoration. "As far as I'm concerned, and I think most of my colleagues in the non-profit area would agree, *restoration* means taking material from several different sources, comparing it, and then producing a new, more complete, or a better-looking version of the film."   —*Jan-Christopher Horak*

Restoration goes beyond the physical copying of surviving material into the reconstruction of the most authentic version of a film. Ideally, this requires comparison of all surviving material on a given title, consultation of printed records of the production and exhibition history, and then decisions regarding the film's "original" state.

Safety stock. See under **base**.

Second generation. See **fine-grain master positive** and **lavender positive**.

Separations. See **YCMs**.

Shrinkage. Usually refers to linear shrinkage along the length of the film. Modern printers can accommodate for as much as 3 percent shrinkage in length.

Third generation. See **duplicate ("dupe") negative** and **preprint materials**.

Timing. See under **prints**.

Viewing print. See under **prints**.

Wet printer. See **wet-gate printer**.

Wet-gate printer. Also known as *liquid-gate printer* and *wet printer*. Printer in which the film to be copied (the *preprint material*) is wetted by a solvent solution that cleans the film and removes superficial scratches. It passes through an aquarium-type of mechanism that both applies the solvent and takes it off. The raw stock does not become wet. Wet-gate can be used with *step printers* (or *optical printers*) that have a lens between the pieces of film. The light source is behind the preprint material, shooting through to the raw stock.

YCMs. Also known as *yellow-cyan-magenta* and *separations*. Eastman Color negatives, if not properly stored, can fade in just a few years. To protect against this, preservationists create a *YCM*—three strips of film called *separations* that divide the color spectrum into yellow, cyan, and magenta. In this widely used process, color film is copied through red, blue, and green filters to create three separate black-and-white records. When a new print is generated the original color is re-created by printing the three positives as one onto color stock. Since black-and-white stock cannot fade, the color negative is protected.

In theory, recombining the separations is a simple matter. In practice, there are frequent problems, often because the separations were not tested when they were made.

In 1995 full testing of color separations ran between $25,000 and $40,000 for a two-hour feature. This doubles the initial cost of making the YCMs. It is more common for a studio to make a test print of a few hundred feet. This costs only about seven hundred dollars.

However, not fully testing separations can be an expensive gamble when a studio finds out they do not have proper protection for their faded Eastman Color negatives.

In 1980 *Daily Variety* estimated that about 20 percent of producers made separations and that they were routinely made at Paramount, Universal, and Disney, which has long made two sets of black-and-white separation masters, storing one in a Kansas salt mine.

Today, in response to the color-fading problem, more and more films are being protected with color separations. In the past, however, most studios made YCMs selectively—just for pictures likely to be re-released. Twentieth Century–Fox, for example, made black-and-white separations of the George Lukas mega-hits *Star Wars* (1977) and *The Empire Strikes Back* (1980), but did not immediately make them for *Norma Rae* (1979), for which Sally Field won the Oscar for Best Actress.

Internet Resources

Facts about film preservation and restoration are plentiful on the Internet. Currently the major archives, as well as many other related cultural organizations, have home pages offering up-to-date details about the field. The Library of Congress's National Film Preservation Board site lists worldwide links for film and video archives, schools, and associations.

American Film Institute
http://www.afionline.org/

International Museum of Photography and Film at George Eastman House
http://www.it.rit.edu/~gehouse/

Library of Congress National Film Preservation Board
http://lcweb.loc.gov/film/

Museum of Modern Art Department of Film and Video
http://www.moma.org/filmvideo.html

UCLA Film and Television Archive
http://www.cinema.ucla.edu/

Suggested Reading

Barry, Iris. "The Film Library and How It Grew." *Film Quarterly* 22 (Summer 1969).

Behlmer, Rudy. *Behind the Scenes: The Making of . . ..* Hollywood: Samuel French, 1989.

————. "*The Black Pirate*: High Style on the High Seas." *American Cinematographer* 73 (April 1992).

————. "*The Black Pirate* Weighs Anchor." *American Cinematographer* 73 (May 1992).

Brownlow, Kevin. "*Napoleon*": *Abel Gance's Classic Film.* New York: Alfred A. Knopf, 1983.

Everson, William K. *American Silent Film.* New York: Oxford University Press, 1978.

Fisher, Bob. "Off to Work We Go: The Digital Restoration of 'Snow White.'" *American Cinematographer* 74 (September 1993).

Francis, David. "Film Conservation Center: A Pioneer in Saving Movies." *Library of Congress Information Bulletin* 50 (January 14, 1991).

Frank, Sam. "*Lost Horizon* Losses Restored." *American Cinematographer* 68 (July 1987).

Gitt, Robert, and Richard Dayton. "Restoring *Becky Sharp*." *American Cinematographer* 65 (November 1984).

Gunning, Tom. "Rebirth of a Movie: How the Museum of Modern Art Restored Griffith's *Way Down East*." *American Film* 10 (October 1984).

Haver, Ronald. "*A Star Is Born*": *The Making of the 1954 Movie and Its 1983 Restoration.* New York: Harper & Row, 1990.

Houston, Penelope. *Keepers of the Frame: The Film Archives.* London: The British Film Institute, 1994.

Karr, Lawrence F. "Film Preservation: Why Nitrate Won't Wait." *I.A.T.S.E. Official Bulletin*, no. 477 (Summer 1972).

Katz, Ephraim. *The Film Encyclopedia.* New York: HarperCollins, 1994.

Lax, Eric. *Woody Allen: A Biography.* New York: Vintage Books, 1992.

McBride, Joseph. "Wise Move Raises *Kane* For Viewers." *Daily Variety*, May 1, 1991.

MacQueen, Scott. "*Doctor X*—a Technicolor Landmark." *American Cinematographer* 67 (June 1986).

———. "*Snow White and the Seven Dwarfs:* Epic Animation Restored." *The Perfect Vision* 6 (July 1994).

May, Richard P. "Scarlet Returns in a Refreshed *GWTW*." *American Cinematographer* 70 (April 1989).

Melville, Annette, and Scott Simmon. *Film Preservation 1993: A Study of the Current State of American Film Preservation.* Report of the Librarian of Congress. 4 vols. Washington, D.C.: Library of Congress, 1993.

———. *Redefining Film Preservation: A National Plan: Recommendations of the Librarian of Congress in Consultation with the National Film Preservation Board.* Washington, D.C.: Library of Congress, August 1994.

Morris, L. Robert, and Lawrence Raskin. *"Lawrence of Arabia": The 30th Anniversary Pictorial History.* New York: Anchor Books, 1992.

Sargent, Ralph. *Preserving the Moving Image.* Washington, D.C.: Corporation for Public Broadcasting/National Endowment for the Arts, 1974.

Sheehan, Henry. "The Fall and Rise of *Spartacus*." *Film Comment* 27 (March–April 1991).

Slide, Anthony. *Nitrate Won't Wait: Film Preservation in the United States.* Jefferson, N.C.: McFarland & Company, Inc., 1992.

Spehr, Paul C. "The Color Film Crisis." *American Film* 5 (November 1979).

Spotnitz, Frank. "Riddle of the Archives." *American Film* 15 (April 1990).

Stevenson, William. "Cutting Remarks." *Film Comment* 26 (July–August 1990).

Thompson, Frank. *Lost Films: Important Movies That Disappeared.* New York: Citadel Press, 1996.

Truffaut, François. *The Films in My Life.* Trans. Leonard Mayhew. New York: Simon and Schuster, 1978.

Index

About the Authors

Joanne L. Yeck earned her Ph.D. in film history and criticism from the University of Southern California. She has written dozens of articles about classic Hollywood for a variety of publications, as well as contributing to the writing of several books on motion pictures, including *The RKO Story, Evenings with Cary Grant,* and *The American Film Institute Catalogue 1931–1940.* **Tom Mc Greevey** is an actor-turned-writer. Together they co-authored *Movie Westerns* (1994). Yeck and Mc Greevey are married to each other and share the rearing of their daughter, Zan, in Santa Fe, New Mexico.